Home on the Urban Range

Home on the Urban Range
An idea map for reforming the city

by **Filip Palda**

The Fraser Institute

Vancouver, British Columbia, Canada

Printed and bound in Canada.

Canadian Cataloguing in Publication Data

Palda, Filip (K. Filip)

Home on the Urban Range

Includes bibliographical references.
ISBN 0-88975-186-2

1. Urban economics. 2. Privatization. I. Fraser Institute (Vancouver, B.C.) II. Title.
HT321.P34 1998   330.9137'2   C98-910944-5

Dedication

Inscribed to the inspiring memory of Milada Randaccio.

Acknowledgements

I thank Michel Boucher of the École nationale d'administration publique in Quebec, and Herbert Grubel of Simon Fraser University for excellent comments on earlier drafts of this book. I also thank two anonymous referees for their excellent insights. Their comments helped more than they can know.

Contents

one
WELCOME
to the
JUNGLE

> When constant wars made the Roman treasury run
> short, our forefathers often used to levy a property
> tax. Every effort must be made to prevent a repetition
> of this; and all possible precautions must be taken to
> ensure that such a step will never be needed.
> —Cicero, *On Duties*

I AM SITTING IN A RESTAURANT DOWNTOWN. The feast is over and reality is about to sink its fangs into my wallet. Why does a plate of nachos cost ten dollars? Am I hallucinating when I read that coffee here sells for three dollars a cup? My study of economics tells me that restaurants are competitive. So these prices cannot be blamed on the owner's greed. If he tries to gouge customers, greedy competitors down the street will steal his business by charging less. Some other force is at work. I reach into my briefcase for a copy of "Business Property Taxation" and find a clue. This study by Harry Kitchen and Enid Slack looks at who benefits from local government spending and who pays the price. In their survey of eight Ontario municipalities they found that businesses pay on average twice as much in local taxes as the city spends on them. Punitive taxes force businesses to subsidize the citizen's utilities, garbage, road, police, parks, and education. But the buck does not stop there. Businesses pass it on. When I drink coffee I am drinking taxes. The hot sauce on those nachos is pure *impuesto* (the Spanish word for tax). Without Kitchen and Slack's insights, I might still think the taxes on my house are reasonable for the services I get. I might still be glad that businesses are paying for local schools and maintaining the city. Now I know these were foolish thoughts. The tax bill I receive and the taxes I pay are not the same. City taxes hide behind every hotdog stand and swirl with the cream in every coffee cup. I feel like Charles Ryder, the hero of *Brideshead Revisited*, who declares, "From then on I would live in the world of three dimensions, with only the aid of my five senses. I have since discovered that there is no such world." In modern city government, as in Castle Howard, nothing is at it seems to be.

The Invisible Tax Collector

I hand the waiter my money under the phantom of the tax collector hovering above us. Something is wrong here. City taxes should not masquerade as ordinary prices. The masquerade makes it hard for voters to tell what kind of a job their local politicians are doing. Am I getting good value for my taxes? Hard to tell, if I don't know my true tax bill. How much of my restaurant tab should I blame on the business property tax? I cannot know that a slice of the food bill meets the union demands of public school teachers, feeds revellers at the city's New Year levee, and supports avant-garde artists living on city grants. My ignorance does not allow me to see what politicians are up to with my money. This ignorance allows politicians to be invisible. According to the ancient Greeks, a shepherd named Giges discovered a ring that made him invisible. By murdering his enemies and confusing subjects of the kingdom, Giges took the throne of Lydia, where he tyrannized the people with his special power. Property taxes on business are like a cloak of invisibility, allowing politicians to blunder and bend to the demands of special interests.

Spoiling a Good Thing

Most cities have gone down this dark road of imposing hidden taxes, and down others I hope to explore. Maybe that's inevitable. All good things spoil, and cities are a very good thing. Why should the spoiling of cities be a given? Let us review the facts.

A city is above all a place where people meet to cooperate in their self-interest. To paraphrase a Middle-Eastern prophet from the old days, "Wherever two people meet in the name of self-interest, let that place be called a market." A market is a place where people come to exchange ideas, goods and services, and to gossip. Sometimes they go just to window shop. It's fun and it helps them become better buyers next time they come to market. Because exchanges are mostly voluntary, they create wealth. Why would two people trade something unless they each had something to gain? The wealth that is created is the difference between what it costs to provide my cup of coffee and the value I place on that coffee. Forget taxes for a moment and calculate that for each cup he sells, it costs my restaurateur 25 cents to buy the raw ingredients, heat them, pay for the espresso machine, rent the premises, pay the waiter, and manage the whole affair. I am a big espresso fan and if you pushed me I might pay up to five dollars a cup. The difference between what I am willing to pay and what it costs the restaurateur is the wealth or "surplus" created by the exchange, in this case $4.75. Not all exchanges lead to a big surplus. Someone who values espresso at 25 cents a cup gets so little value for his money that the exchange creates no wealth. If I blunder into a poorly managed restaurant where it costs $5 to produce a cup, there is again nothing to be gained from the exchange. The surplus that can be generated from an efficient producer is like honey. Like honey, the surplus attracts beekeepers and bears.

How Cities Create Wealth

Beekeepers are the people who organize markets. Their wealth comes from matching the people who value a good highly with those who can produce it at low cost. Matching sounds boring and without value, until you peek under the intellectual covers of market economics. There is a reason why 70 percent of national wealth is attributed to the service industry. This industry is largely about matching means to needs. Bank workers, the poster children of the service industry, are matchmakers. They take money from people willing to lend at a low rate and make it available to people who are willing to pay a great deal to borrow and invest the money in some profitable scheme. Sears, Eatons, Bloomingdales, and other large department stores are also expert matchmakers. They send purchasing agents to Asia to find low-cost furniture and contract to have stock brought to North America for the pleasure of those with a taste for such things. Middlemen make the market. Their reward is a cut of the surplus generated between both ends of that market—me the consumer, and some distant producer.

Cities can generate fortunes from matchmaking, without ever producing and exporting a single physical product. This is the message that comes from historian R.C. Michie's study of the world food trade at the turn of the century. In the early part of the century, London rose to prominence by becoming a clearing house for foodstuffs from around the world. As Michie explains, "London's combination of expertise, organization and convenience made it a popular entrepôt to which foods could be shipped and stored before dispatch to a final destination, as was often required by seasonally produced crops. Many bulky commodities also required careful inspection and quality testing before sale to users, such as in the case of coffee or tea, and London was one of the few centres where such a facility was available." Gradually, London lost its advantage as a port of transshipment and inspection, but maintained its leadership in the foodstuff business by becoming the world centre for food brokering. Commodities traders in London helped finance and buffer the risks of food shipments between countries. "Plantation companies producing tea, rice, spices and rubber, whatever the origin of their founders, found it convenient to establish either branches or connections in London, through which their products could be marketed and their supplies obtained." Eventually, London's part in the world food trade developed into a meeting place where people could match the need of producers and consumers around the world. As Michie writes with insight, "This move from the physical to the office trade was missed by most contemporaries who only saw Britain being by-passed by cargoes that were once transshipped there.... Consequently, historians have failed to appreciate the transformation in trade while economists tend to ignore the importance of intermediation and organization." Safe, orderly trade is what cities are about.

Markets do more than match goods and consumers. They match workers with employers. The costs of not getting the match right are high. The effort to avoid such costs are at the heart of David Mamet's play *Glengarry Glen Ross*. The head office of the real estate company, Mitch and Murray, has to decide which agents will get the "leads." Leads are potential buyers the agency has researched. The most promising leads are matched, through a miasma of profane dialogue, to the best agents. This resembles how marriage markets work. The best prospects seek each other out to amplify each other's aptitudes, generate the best offspring, and make the most money. Friends, social clubs, and any activity that takes more than one person, benefits from sound matching.

Make Me a Match

Where do cities come in? Talk about a meeting place. Where else can you sleep, eat, work, and shop in a thousand places? Cities are SUPER markets. They are humankind's solution to the problem of distance. Distance is the enemy of trade. It is expensive to travel to exchange your products. It is cheaper to live in the market, where

customers and suppliers are closely packed. The earliest city arose
not for security—it is much safer to cower in a bush than make yourself a rich target for marauders—but because of the good things that
came from living close to the market. Roman architects managed to
raise apartments to about five stories. This technological innovation
helped Rome condense a million people into a few hundred football
fields and become the market capital of the ancient world. Cities got
another boost in 1850 when Otis invented the "safety lift." What soon
became known as the elevator allowed William Lebaron Jenney to
build the first iron-frame skyscrapers. Technology annihilates distance, the enemy of markets.

With little distance to travel, consumers can shop. This means com-
paring prices and the quality of goods. Honest merchants who think
they have something special to offer often cluster in specialized malls
where consumers can judge what these merchants have to offer. As
early as the 1890s on South Michigan Street in Chicago, car vendors
clustered. You can still see these buildings with their modernistic
Chicago architecture and porcelain tile logos advertising the "Loco-
mobile," as the car was once called. Without cities there would be no
clustering. These clusters are like magnets for enterprises that may be
located thousands of miles away. The city is a clearing house and dis-
play case for everything good that dispersed people have to offer.
This is how cities contribute to international trade and how international trade invigorates cities.

Without modern cities there would be no permanence. Permanence
is the bedrock of honesty in commerce. In the old days, people lived
in settlements too small for a merchant class to settle in. Merchants
solved this problem by inventing the caravan. A caravan was a moving market that travelled to many small cities in an effort to simulate
the economic effects of trading in a single large metropolis. Certain
microorganisms also need a critical mass to propagate. They use a
technique similar to the caravan. Chicken pox is an example. It
strikes in youth, and returns in 50 years as shingles, travelling across

time and down nerve ending, like pack-camels across the desert, to invade a new host of youngsters.

Travel helped caravans overcome the problem of a critical mass of consumers, but also introduced the problem of dishonesty. In a moving market, the consumer who gets cheated cannot go back to complain. Neither can he use the information of his "burn" to make a better purchase next time. This makes it difficult to tell an honest merchant from a fraud and stifles consumer demand. Cities allow honest merchants to thrive by allowing them to park their caravans permanently in a shop, department store, or head office. With these honest merchants in place, consumers are willing to risk the purchase of new products without too much fear of bamboozlement.

In talking about matching, I may sound like the host of *The Dating Game*, a 1960s television program in which a woman posed questions to three men fidgeting behind a daisy-covered screen. This is the tone I want to set. In the dating game the variety of candidates meant that anything could happen. The same is true in the city. As Mark Twain observed on visiting Chicago in 1883, "[it is] a city where they are always rubbing the lamp and fetching up the genie, and contriving and achieving new impossibilities. It is hopeless for the occasional visitor to try to keep up with Chicago—she outgrows his prophecies faster than he can make them. She is always a novelty; for she is never the Chicago you saw when you passed through last time."

Less Hardware for More People

The advantages of city life are compounded by the fact that living in densely populated communities is cheap. The most widely cited study on the matter is a 1974 treatise published by the US government. *The Costs of Sprawl* is the Manhattan Project of urban research. The idea behind this work was to give local planners a sense of what it costs to provide services to high-density and low-density areas. The conclusions of this intellectual A-bomb were that "Sprawl is the most expensive form of residential development in terms of economic costs, environmental costs, natural resource consumption, and many types of personal costs . . . while planning results in cost savings, density is a much more influential cost determinant . . . Compared to low density sprawl, the amount of total capital costs borne by local government may decrease by almost 50 percent for high density planned communities. Operating and maintenance costs borne by local government may decrease by 13 percent." The study also found that increasing density from two to ten dwellings per acre (a fivefold increase) only doubled government's capital costs. Density eliminates "leapfrogging" which involves costly road and utility connections between neighbourhoods. Less pipework, twisted around fewer bends for an apartment block, explains part of the difference in costs.

A conclusive verdict is still out on the issues of sprawl and the cost of police, but it may also be cheaper to police and protect one concentrated apartment building than to patrol ten suburban houses spread over a block. The same logic applies to fire protection. Garbage collection is cheaper in concentrated neighbourhoods and pollution of many sorts is lower than in sprawling neighbourhoods. Air pollution from cars is 50 percent lower, pollution from space heating is 40 percent lower. Open spaces are conserved in dense communities, and wildlife is protected. Less soil gets churned up in building a dense community, so that dirty water run-off from storms is 20 percent less than in sprawl. And 40 percent less water gets used in dense communities because there are fewer lawns to water. Sprawling suburbs suffer from the additional costs that come from having to build massive expressways to carry suburbanites to work downtown. This difference in costs is why, at the turn of the century, before governments hid these costs, the suburbs were where the rich lived. Only the wealthy could afford the high cost of living on the outskirts.

Hey! You've Got to Hide Your Costs Away

Today, governments hide the benefits we get from living close together. They do this by refusing to charge citizens directly for the services they use. Instead, the favourite means of finance is to get everyone to put money into a central pot. In Canada, cities get on average 45 percent of their money from higher levels of government, and 40 percent from property taxes. Only 11 percent of revenues come from user fees that show citizens the true costs of their demands upon the city. For example, services such as transportation and roads are provided by provincial governments.

Central financing has flattened the city as would a bomb. One reason why homeowners fled to the suburbs was to avoid paying for other people's consumption of city services. Property taxes are based on a house's assessed value. This means that owners of inexpensive houses pay less for the same city services as owners of expensive houses. They put less into the central pot but get the same services out of government. Someone has to pick up their tab. Part is picked up by subsidies from higher levels of government (i.e. unsuspecting citizens living perhaps a thousand miles away). Another part is paid by the property taxes of people living nearby in expensive houses.

The easiest way to protect owners of expensive houses from being taken for a ride would be to charge directly for city services. But the politics of charging user fees proved too difficult, so to protect their wallets, central city dwellers fled to suburban communities with different tax laws. To stop owners of low-cost dwellings from following them to the suburbs, owners of high-cost dwellings have passed zoning laws limiting how many people you can cram onto a parcel of land. This raises the cost of housing and keeps away the free-riders. Zoning institutionalizes sprawl. Sprawl has been reinforced by the fact that cities do not charge their citizens directly for the use of streets. Edwin Mills of Northwestern University and Bruce Hamilton of Johns Hopkins University estimate that if people in the US paid directly for their use of roads, the proportion of people living in city centres would rise from 47.5 percent to 59 percent.

Why, in spite of the damage central financing does to cities, do governments allow some citizens a free ride on the tax money of others? The answer has to do with the surplus I mentioned earlier. Cities are the flagships of markets. They are the pride of the economic fleet because they match people who want something badly with those who can produce it efficiently. This match-up produces what economists call a surplus. You can also think of it as honey.

The tremendous potential for honey causes cities to grow and attract the finest market minds. This surplus has also attracted bears who want to skim some of the sweet stuff for themselves. Bears know that you can take from the bees, give nothing back, and have a feast. This does not mean that bears get their meals for free. They will get stung on the nose and fight off other bears for their meal of honey. The bears of the city are interest groups of citizens who want others to pay for their lifestyle and who lobby to get their way.

"Thar Be Pickin's For All"

Where are these bears? Think of yourself and your neighbour. Both of you pay the same property tax, but he puts out twice as much garbage as you, washes his car three times a week (you don't have a car), and calls the police at least once a month for fear that someone is breaking in to get at what he believes is a valuable collection of baseball cards. Both of you pay the same flat city tax rate but he is a public services glutton. It's the same sort of redistribution that happens at smorgasbords. Nibblers subsidize the big eaters. The main difference between smorgasbord restaurants and the city is that going to the restaurant is voluntary. Mostly big eaters go. In the end the price adjusts so that no one gets a free ride. It is harder to escape the city than to avoid a restaurant. Where there is no escape, some citizens will pay so that others can play.

The amount of money that changes hands by government force would have aroused envy in those marauders of the Sumer who swept down on a city, took what they could get their hands on, and rode away burdened with treasure. These days, things are not so rowdy. That is because money drawn from a central pot obscures the reality of who pays and who benefits. An interest group that wants money does not hold the taxpayers who must pay the bill at spear point. The group gets government to do the dirty work. This detour removes those who pay the interest group from the interest group's sight.

Nobel prizewinning physician Konrad Lorenz suggested that the invention of long-range methods of killing had a similar effect on soldiers. Pilots in the Second World War could not have shot an enemy child at close range with a pistol. From a height of 40,000 feet, killing hundreds of children in a single run became a more bearable abstraction. Central financing of city government puts a similar distance between interest groups and those who pay for their well-being. This distance loosens inhibitions about receiving favours from government. Frederic Bastiat, a French economist of the 19th century, put the problem as follows:

> The oppressor no longer acts directly by his own force on the oppressed. No, our conscience has become too fastidious for that. There are still, to be sure, the oppressor and his victim, but between them is placed an intermediary, the state. What is better fitted to silence our scruples and to overcome all resistance?

Bastiat is saying that devious forms of redistribution bring out a bit of the marauder in all of us. The only difference between me and the raider is that I don't cap my flowing mane with a bronze helmet, nor do I burst out the front door after breakfast with shield and sword, ready to plunder. As pleasing as these thoughts might sometimes be, I don't need to play them out. I have government to do the marauding for me. The result is, as the Roman statesman Seneca bemoaned, that "In the meanwhile, while they are robbing and being robbed, while they disrupt each other's repose and make one another miserable, life remains without profit, without pleasure, without moral improvement."

Put more crudely, the surplus of wealth that cities generate pulls people away from productive activities and leads them to plunder each other's wealth with government's help. These battles make nonsense of what a city should be. Cities exist to concentrate people in narrow, organized spaces. Property taxes, subsidies and other assaults undo this organization. The urban sprawl of the modern city is a sign of the chaos brought on by government policies that cut the link between how people live in the city and the cost of living. We clog roads, infest landfills with our garbage, and waste water because government allows us to do so without direct charge. Politicians have turned the city into a pasture where citizens feed at each other's cost without restraint and lead the city away from the efficient, concentrated form nature intended.

Many have warned against the dangers of allowing government to set us against one another. Cicero put it this way, "For if each of us proposes to rob or injure one another for our personal gain, then we are clearly going to demolish the link that unites every human being with every other. Just imagine if each of our limbs had its own consciousness and saw advantage for itself in appropriating the nearest limb's strength! Of course our whole body would inevitably collapse and die. In precisely the same way, a general seizure and appropriation of other people's property would cause the collapse of the human community."

Head in the Sand

The way to rid cities of this economic pest is to recognize that there is a problem. Most people I have spoken to say they are by and large happy with city governments. I can't blame them for being complacent. How many of us know any city government other than the ones we have grown up with? As the rulers of the Soviet Union understood, ignorance is bliss. When voters are kept in the dark about their alternatives from the start, their expectations are tiny, and they don't grow up whiny.

Democratic systems are not as good as dictatorships at blocking information about alternatives, but they try. Democratic politicians tend to resist changes in city administration that would allow voters to grasp where their money is going. This is why user fees play so small a role in the financing of cities. In Canada 11 percent of city services are funded by user fees (22 percent if education and social welfare are not counted as city services). The remainder comes from property taxes and provincial subsidies. The city's reliance on property taxes and subsidies creates a fog in the city voter's brain. User fees would lift that fog because they provide information.

A user fee is like a price. Prices reveal several things about the good in question. In a competitive climate prices show whether the producer is doing a good job of keeping costs down. Now, think of a city in which departments are run as separate governments, each with its own budget. The garbage government would charge private citizens a user fee. If this government was not good at its job, the user fee would rise and send a signal to voters that it is time for a change. No other department could come to its aid by slipping it money, as is the case when city services are funded from a central pot of property taxes. No provincial government could come to its aid. User fees would give voters a sense of how well each city department is doing. That sort of savvy citizen makes the difference between a vibrant democracy and the kind of democracy cities now have, in which no more than 40 percent of voters cast ballots.

Information in the user-fee world also flows the other way: not only can users evaluate how suppliers perform, suppliers can evaluate what consumers want. The question that haunts politicians is how much of a public service to provide. Politicians have trouble answering because most local public services are either given free of direct charge or at a subsidized price. The politician finds out whether he provided the right amount of local service only at election time. User fees give leaders instant feedback on how much citizens value a public service. If citizens are made to pay the true price of a bus ride, and half the fleet goes empty, leaders know it is time to sell off some buses. If they do not sell the buses, they must live with the knowledge that they are not matching the needs of their constituents to the resources of the community.

Matching needs to resources is what makes a community grow rich. This is what markets do with the help of prices. Markets are where consumers who value a good seek out producers who can sell it to them at a low price. Prices reveal who is a serious consumer and who is an efficient producer. Without bus fares that reflect the true cost of the service, a community may be going to great lengths to please riders who do not care for what they receive. Such is the folly the Bible warns against, in advising not to scatter pearls before swine.

User fees occupy a tiny part of our minds because no one has done a good job of selling the idea. Politicians are certainly not in favour of the greater transparency of their performance that results from fees. For a sense of how marginal user fees are in the public mind, take a look at a computer game called Sim City. In this million-selling game, you are mayor of an imaginary city. You pass zoning laws, build stadiums, and levy property taxes. There are no user fees for roads, garbage, police, fire, ambulance, public transit, libraries, parks, and water. This game's makers are missing out on something.

Once user fees are explained, people like the idea. What grabs them most is not so much my notion about the information derived from fees, but the fact that user fees can cut your tax bill. All you have to do is be more careful about the amount of garbage you throw out, the water you spray, and other city services you consume. You no longer have to worry about paying for your neighbour's gluttony for city services, and you no longer feel the need to force-feed yourself on these services just to make sure that you are getting some of your property tax dollars back. If people have worries about user fees, these worries are about making sure that the city sets the "right" price for its services. But the right price will not drop from heaven. Right prices result only from a climate of competition. This climate is absent in most cities because municipal unions provide the services and prevent competition. Opening city services to competitive tender from private suppliers would reduce these unions' ability to feed on citizens' tax dollar.

We do not have a city in which user fees direct our actions and promote a respect for property because politicians at higher levels of government have not wished it. If citizens understood the true cost of local government they would demand more control over it. Provincial governments and the federal capital would be at risk of losing power to communities. This is why leaders at these levels speak with religious fervour about the need to maintain universal social services and to harmonize the tax system. These arrangements put higher levels of government in the driver's seat and leave communities with little to do but follow orders from on high. The challenge to citizens is to increase power at the community level. At this level citizens will be able to use government to protect property. Because, yes, we do need government.

The Role of Government

A city needs government, just as a country club needs an administrative board. Both the city and the country club need to avoid and settle disputes over how people use common areas. Without government the city would fall into chaos. To enforce its will, the city needs arbitrary powers over property. These powers include the power to tax, regulate, and zone. The challenge to citizens is to contain these powers. Arbitrary is another way of saying "up for grabs." If city employees make their grab by trying to charge a high price for city services, it is not because they are evil or lazy. We and other city dwellers who prey on each other through the tax system are not vampires. Suburbanites, city unions, and anyone else who exploits the resources of the city that are up for grabs are just doing what they must to survive. That the result is evil is the fault of a system in which power is left concentrated and unsupervised.

As I leave the restaurant I look back at the placemat where I doodled these grand thoughts. The busboy is clearing the table and putting down a new placemat. If only we could do the same for the city. Where would we start? The answer is as close as the pavement under my feet.

Read On ...

Bastiat, Frederic. "Government." In *Essays on Political Economy*, by Frederic Bastiat. London: Provost and Co. 1875, pages 119-135.

Grant, Michael. *Cicero: Selected Works*. London: Penguin Books, 1960.

Hadas, Moses. *The Stoic Philosophy of Seneca: Essays and Letters*. New York: W.W. Norton & Company, 1958.

Kitchen, Harry M. and Enid Slack. "Business Property Taxation." Discussion Paper 93-24, Queen's University School of Policy Studies, 1993.

Michie, R.C. (1996). "The International Trade in Food and the City of London Since 1850." *European Journal of Economic History*, 25: 369-404.

Real Estate Research Corporation. *The Costs of Sprawl: Environmental and Economic Costs of Alternative Residential Development*

Patterns at the Urban Fringe. Washington D.C.: United States Government Printing Office, (1974).

Mills, Edwin S. and Bruce W. Hamilton. *Urban Economics,* 4th ed. Boston: Scott, Foresman and Company, 1989.

two
MAD MAX
at the
TOLL BOOTH

The freeway [is] a contradiction in terms in Los Angeles.... The original concept of a fast road, free of obstacles, parked cars and traffic lights, has long since faded from popular thinking. For Angelenos, a freeway means a free-for-all, where junk, manners and lane discipline can be jettisoned willy-nilly, and where free means free: gratis, for nothing.
—*Financial Times of London*, Dec. 23, 1997

I DRIVE MY CAR AWAY FROM THE RESTAURANT AND ON TO THE ROAD. A tap on the accelerator leaves smears of rubber on the asphalt and startles passers-by. This must have been how cowboys felt. Today, streets and expressways are the best places to recapture the feeling of the open plain. Streets are the Wild West of the modern city. Correction. Streets are better than the West. Here there is no Wyatt Earp. There are police who sometimes stop drunk drivers and pull apart angry motorists at the scene of a fender-bender. But there are no police for that enduring offence against city development: rush hour.

Don't Blame Cars

The media love to blame congested streets on the automobile. This is like blaming the carving knife for cutting your finger. Cars are not to blame for clogged urban arteries. The culprits are the rules governing those cars. The present rules are simple: everyone drives when they want, at no direct charge. The cost is covered by property owners, gasoline taxes, and subsidies from higher governments. Some excess traffic is taken care of by government transit monopolies that survive on transfusions of taxpayer support. At every turn, governments hide the true cost of travel and pick some pockets to stuff others. In so doing, they encourage a smorgasbord of driving, with side dishes of generous pay for unions of transit employees. Here is what Nobel prizewinning economist William Vickerey had to say—between bouts of pulling out his hair—about the system: "In no other major area are pricing practices so irrational, so out of date, and so conducive to waste as in urban transportation." If cities are to get another shot at greatness, transportation is the place to start tinkering.

Why get upset about rush hour? Think about the costs. The costs of running into rush hour are as varied as the people who get caught in one. Bakeries pay drivers to sit in traffic. Commuters ask for wages that compensate them for the 40 minutes of travel between home and work. Shoppers waste time in traffic jams they could spend in the mall. This lost time gets subtracted from the time they can devote to maintaining a house or relaxing.

Cities suffer from slow traffic the way computer programs suffer from a slow chip. Cities are three-dimensional computer chips through which human electrons move in their search for goods and services that match their needs. Matching is difficult in a city that slows down the search. Those who dwell in a slow-moving city suffer as Robinson Crusoe suffered. Without others to help him and trade with him, he was stuck with what his two hands could produce. In a city where trade is not profitable, citizens will not invest in the "institutions" of trade. Crusoe did not build a trading post or a stock exchange because there was no one to exchange with. In a city where traffic is slow, people are slow to invest in markets. A Bloomingdales or a Sears, which are both markets, wants to locate where people are. They want to be at the crossroads of everyone's trip. The city stops being a crossroads if the roads to downtown are plugged. The slow city computer has led department stores to set up in the suburbs where they form mini-centres. Mini-centres may seem like a smart way of solving the traffic jam problem. Instead, they are a sign of how the users of a slow computer can rewire the system for the worse. The commercial diaspora to the suburbs eases the traffic jam problem, but at a cost. Instead of having one centre where all goods can be found and prices can be compared, we waste time travelling between mini-centres for the same information.

The costs of congestion add up to more than slow traffic. In traffic jams we learn to despise humanity and to mistrust the benefits of co-operation. Look at what happens when you play the good citizen in such a jam. Suppose that you realize roads would be better with fewer cars on them and decide to pull off at the next exit and park at the curb for 30 minutes. The space you have just freed is now open to someone zooming down the next feeder ramp. He will not see or understand your sacrifice but will instead just fill the space you have liberated. He may be a criminal, a drunk, or just someone you would not be inclined to go out of your way to help. The science of psychology tells us that behaviour is reinforced by positive feedback. There is no such feedback in the traffic jam. You cannot offer your help to deserving people and you get no thanks.

Consider the flip side. You join traffic that is flowing slowly and on the verge of logjam. You get on the expressway and slow a thousand cars behind you by a second. This works out to 16.7 minutes lost to others. Your cost is minimal. And you don't see the victims, which could include a mother on her way to delivery, a student on the way to exams, or a senior on his way to the emergency room. So it's easy to

convince yourself that what you are doing is OK. Inconsiderate behaviour thrives without negative feedback. People are not naturally
bad, but they can find themselves in circumstances where they are
forced to behave badly. These circumstances do not allow people to
coordinate their actions for the common good. Coordination means
that people are not stepping on each other's faces.

Lack of such coordination is responsible for ecological disasters,
such as the near extinction of the buffalo. The pioneer with his gun-
sights on the buffalo might have been a conservationist at heart, but
he had to ask himself a question: "If I don't shoot this creature, will
my restraint allow it to grow, have offspring, and populate nature?"
The answer was no. His restraint would simply make an extra buffalo
available for someone else to shoot. That someone else might also
have been a conservationist but in the great anonymous rush of pio-
neers to the West, you had to assume the worst. The result was that a
normally restrained people ended up doing serious damage to nature.
Today we have learned that there are several ways to preserve nature.
One of the most successful is to charge hunters and fishermen a fee
for each animal they catch. These fees limit the hunt and go toward
preserving the lakes and forests.

Why the above-mentioned fees? In the old days, people were tied to
the land. Keeping to one place and knowing your neighbour allowed
traditions for preserving nature to develop. When the Native peoples
first came from Asia to North America across the frozen passage, it is
possible they annihilated the sloth, mammoth, horse, and sabre-
toothed tiger. After they settled they learned the value of preserving
nature and developed traditions and religions of conservation. Religions that worship nature have, of course, a strong spiritual side, but it
is hard to ignore their practical side. These religions result from generations of trial and error and preach sound ecological management.
The golden rule guiding many religions and philosophies is ecological: do unto others as you would have them do unto you. In other

words, act by taking into account the cost your use of resources imposes on other people.

In an anonymous, fast-moving society the golden rule gets overlooked. Nobody knows what others are up to, so that the rule's social sanctions and rewards do not come into play. After a while, people who obey the rule get tired of being taken advantage of by the anonymous violators. A free-for-all follows. It's like the meal eaten by 100 people on a single tab. If I hold back and eat less than the others, I only save $1/100^{th}$ of the expense. The remaining savings are spread among the others. If I indulge, I only pay $1/100^{th}$ of the cost. The mathematics of a single tab equate to an unwanted feast. One way to control the feast is to make everyone pay the cost he would impose on others. In other words, charge him for what he eats. This is what user fees are all about. A user fee imposes the golden rule on thousands of people who don't know each other and have no relation to each other. The price you pay should equal the damage you do to all others when taking something out of the environment for yourself.

User fees for roads would force trucks to use off-street facilities for loading and unloading. Although trucks make up 20 percent of urban travel, they contribute more than their fair share to congestion. US economist Edwin Mills suggests a truck driving downtown at rush hour imposes $30 per hour on others. Currently, trucks do not need to worry about these costs because they do not pay for them. A study of Toronto's city centre found that 19 per cent of freight-vehicle stops were made in front of buildings with good off-street loading facilities, but less than 10 per cent of these trucks made use of those facilities. They could not be bothered because of the small inconvenience of driving off the street. A golden-rule toll of $30 an hour would make off-street loading bays popular places. A user fee would also force private individuals to ask themselves whether they really need to be on the road. The fee would sift serious users from users who can wait an hour or travel an hour earlier. We sift and sort users in this way when it comes to electricity, telephones, and water use. Roads deserve the same treatment.

False Prophets

Before we can devise a workable system of road tolls, we have to rid ourselves of policies that don't work. Gasoline taxes, special license plates, and high parking fees cannot substitute for tolls. Governments who tax gasoline show a poor grasp of the need to charge for road use. Such a tax has a tendency to reduce driving at all times. It does nothing for the problem of rush hours. You pay the tax whether you drive at 5 a.m. or 5 p.m. High parking fees do nothing to discourage the approximately $\frac{1}{3}$ to $\frac{1}{2}$ of rush hour drivers who are simply passing through the city centre. A solution popular in Central and South America is to issue license plates in two colours. On even days one colour drives, while the other colour drives on odd days. Apart from the fact that people cheat by owning two sets of plates, license plate colour does nothing to recognize the differences in value that people attach to their time. People driving with red plates may be as diverse as any you will find in an unregulated system. People who do not need to drive will be mixed in with people in a rush. This is no way to wipe out the blight of the traffic jam. Decongesting roads is not the objective. Decongesting them in a way that only people who most need to be on the road get to drive is the objective. User fees get us there.

The True Light

An intelligent user fee tries to separate the wheat of drivers from the chaff. William Vickerey worked out the details of such a fee as far back as the 1960s. On his ideal road, travellers pay the moment they start rolling. A transponder in the car informs a central city register when and how long the car travelled. Based on this information, the city would send each driver a monthly bill. Drivers could gauge whether it was worth driving by looking at roadside billboards that advertise the cost of travelling at any time. A base fee would apply to driving at any time of day. This fee would be geared towards the costs of building and maintaining the road. To avoid traffic congestion, the fee would rise from this base. As congestion rises, so would prices, until a free flow was once again established on the road. This two-part pricing scheme resembles that found at clubs where users pay a basic entry fee and an additional fee for the use of crowded club facilities.

What would be the best rush hour toll? In the mid-1970s, US economist Theodore Keeler and his colleagues calculated that a rush hour driver imposed 20 cents on other drivers for every mile driven in the suburbs and up to 91 cents for every mile driven downtown. This calculation is made by figuring out how much a car slows all others at rush hour and by attaching a dollar figure to the lost time. Truck drivers imposed up to five dollars per mile or $30 for every hour they spent downtown during the rush hour. These costs are the "optimal tolls" that should be charged. They are optimal in the golden-rule sense because they force drivers to take into account the costs they are imposing on others.

The yearly benefits from tolls would be impressive. Using his computer, Economist Marvin Kraus studied a simulated city of 700,000. He based his computer model on realistic aspects of city geometry, gasoline price, the value of commuter time, and 42 other "parameters" that define a city. This is the sort of exercise familiar to scientists studying the greenhouse effect. They model the winds and rains in a simulated world, based in part on weather readings and in part on equations that tie all the readings together. In Marvin Kraus' simulated city, transponder-tolls improve the average household's well-being by $81.35 a year. A gas tax bringing in an equivalent amount of money would improve well-being by only $58.59 per household.

My guess is that Kraus would have found even greater differences had he allowed households to differ in their time costs. In such a case, tolls would not only decongest roads, they would also sort drivers into hours where people with a low value of time and those with a high value of time do not interfere with each other. Kraus did not model parking surcharges—which are often proposed as a solution to congestion—but noted with disapproval that a parking tax in the downtown allows through-traffic to avoid the tax. "In US cities, it is not uncommon for through-traffic to account for more than half of all central business district traffic."

Street Smarts

In Kraus' model, Vickerey's user fee would force people to ask themselves whether it was really worth their while to travel now or later. The fee would have turned streets from open plains, clogged with herds of unthinking drivers, into polite passageways where every citizen weighs his need to travel against the needs of others. There is nothing new about this idea. Telephone and power companies have been charging "congestion fees" for a hundred years. No one finds it strange that teenagers should wait until midnight to jam the family phone, while executives pay a premium during the day to strike deals over the wire. No one finds it strange that people who use a network should pay for its upkeep. Why should roads be different?

A lack of the technology to bill users is not an excuse for avoiding user fees. The technology to monitor and charge city traffic exists. But, like the moveable type and gunpowder of the ancient Chinese Empire, a question mark hangs over the will of our mandarins to use this technology. In Quebec, tolls *disappeared* from bridges and roads in 1985. Perhaps the wonder is that Quebec ever had tolls in the first place. This province is the most interventionist and subsidy-coddled area of North-America. In Ontario, politicians are less allergic to user fees for certain roads. In 1997 the first 36 kilometres of a 69 kilometre toll highway opened north of Toronto. Drivers who enter Highway

407 have their license plates videotaped. Cameras record where they leave the highway, and a bill is sent to them. Drivers who bother to get an electronic tag for their cars benefit from more convenient billing. Politicians have shown backbone and intelligence by allowing Highway 407 to open equipped with modern billing technology. State Route 91 south of Los Angeles goes further by guaranteeing that tolls will be adjusted so that traffic never clogs.

Expressways seem open to tolls, but when it comes to charging for rides on city streets only a few places on the globe have had the backbone to give Vickerey's idea rein. In the late 1980s, the Norwegian city of Trondheim established a ring of twelve toll-plazas around its centre. Today, 90 per cent of Trondheim's cars are equipped with transponders and drive through these plazas without pausing to pay. They get their bill in the mail or have the cost deducted directly from their bank accounts. Oslo and Bergen have followed suit and other European cities are catching on to the idea. In 1998 Leicester launched the UK's first pay-as-you-go road pricing experiment. Roadside radio beacons deduct value from a smart card fixed to the car windscreen of volunteers in the scheme. Firms with the best technology for billing are becoming big business in Europe.

Little such entrepreneurial spirit is to be found in North American cities. The retrograde thinking of politicians on this side of the herring-pond is to build subsidized transit lines and "high occupancy vehicle lanes" (HOVs) to unclog city streets. Toronto is an example of how such thinking gets applied. In 1996 Toronto councillors voted for a 1 percent increase in property taxes to extend the Sheppard subway line. This works out to an extra $211 million in property taxes over the next six years.

Vancouver matches Toronto in narrow vision. For fear of becoming a northern copy of congested Los Angeles, 20 communities in the Vancouver region joined hands in a non-binding resolution guaranteed to warm the hearts of municipal transit unions, and bus and urban rail builders. The resolution called for millions to be spent upgrading urban transit. About charging for the use of city streets nary a word was heard. Throwing good resources after bad is no novelty. Generals of the Great War showed a similar obduracy. They sent wave after wave of men into machine- gun fire and hesitated to use armoured tanks and bullet-proof vests. User fees are the tanks in the battle against crowded streets, but to date they sit muzzled in the ordnance yard.

Why Resist User Fees?

It may not be fair to blame city politicians for resisting street user fees. User fees are a touchy topic in transportation because voters see them as an added claim on their wallets. Some travellers might be willing to try user fees if they knew that general taxes would fall as user fees rose. But when did taxes ever fall in response to a rise in user fees? These voters are not stupid or mulish in rejecting user fees for roads. They are simply reluctant to let politicians grow another talon for gouging their wallets. Voters might be open to user fees if politicians pledged to make user fees a substitute for taxes, not a complement. In the UK, the opinion among consumer groups such as AA and business groups such as the Freight Transport Association is that road charges would be acceptable to the majority if the revenues were reinvested in improving roads and public transport, or reducing taxes.

Not all voters will be impressed by the promise to replace taxes with user fees. These are voters who believe they benefit from the present system. One such group are citizens who place a low value on their time and live far from the city centre. A low value on time does not mean that these people enjoy life less than others. By value of time, I mean how much pleasure people get from consuming the goods that an hour of work will buy compared to how much joy they get from their leisure. In this sense, if your salary goes up, so does your value of time. This is why people with big salaries attach great value to their time. An hour of their work buys lots of goodies compared to the pleasure they get from loafing. People who have high time-costs will try to live near their place of work, holding all else constant. Citizens with a low value on their time will not mind spending two hours a day in their cars. They lose less consumption than the rich from traffic jams. These are the suburbanites. In his study of the ups and downs of US city development, transport economist James Elliot noted that "Historically, this spill-over of people and jobs to nearby communities has been encouraged by increasing ... government subsidies and infrastructural improvements in the metropolitan fringe." If it is true that the suburbs were built on transport subsidies, politicians will have a rough time selling the idea of user fees to this segment of the population.

The Harm from Subsidies

What harm do subsidies inflict? If suburbanites were made to pay the true cost of building and maintaining roads, as well as the cost of avoiding congestion, some suburbanites would choose to live in city apartments. As mentioned at the start of this book, US economists Edwin Mills and Bruce Hamilton estimate that tolls in the US would increase central-city population from 47.5 percent of total urban population to 59 percent of total urban population.

Without the subsidy, the cost of living in the suburbs would be greater for some people than the benefit. The subsidy does not erase the fact that the costs are greater than the benefits. It simply shifts the costs to someone else. In the world of subsidies, users are from Mars, payers are from Venus, and wealth disappears in the void in between. What else can you expect when you direct resources to people who value those resources at less than cost? The Bible warns against such folly in its exhortation not to throw pearls before swine, lest they trample them under foot, or in this case, under the wheel.

The destruction of wealth through road subsidies would not be possible without the efforts of citizens who create wealth—the "honey" I spoke of earlier. Seeing your wealth destroyed through subsidies is unpleasant. You would think that the people who pay for the pleasure of suburbanites would be up in arms. Instead, their protests are about as forceful as the silence of the lambs. The citizens who pay the cost of suburban excess are silent because they are not aware they are paying these costs. The victims of the subsidy to the suburbs can hardly be blamed for their ignorance. Official propaganda says that expressways are paid for by gasoline taxes. On the surface, it looks like suburbanites pay their fair share of building expressways. They log the most miles on these expressways and so pay more gasoline tax than city dwellers.

A closer look reveals a shell-game. Cities do not collect the gasoline tax. The provinces and the federal government share the tax. They have wide discretion to fund anywhere between 50 percent and 100 percent of road costs. This central collection of revenues and broad discretion in their use is the key to redistributing money in such a way that some people get the roads and others get the tax. It is true that suburbanites will pay more gasoline tax than people who live downtown. This does not mean suburbanites pay the full cost of expressways. Citizens in towns without major suburbs or without expressways connecting suburbs to cities will not require as much transportation subsidy per person from higher levels of government as cities with major expressways. The gasoline tax is blind to the lower cost per mile of building and maintaining the simpler kinds of roads these people use. Whether I travel a mile on a dirt road or a mile on an expressway I pay the same amount in gasoline tax. The province can skim the excess of what I pay to travel the dirt road compared to what it costs to build expressways and use the surplus to subsidize the kinds of roads suburbanites use in major metropolises. In the US, transport economist Robert Poole estimates that "33 states get back less than they contribute in highway taxes and would be better off if funds were left in their states to begin with." The same principle applies to transfers between cities inside a province.

What suburbanites may not realize is that they too pay for their lifestyle. Cities have to maintain the roads that carry herds of suburban drivers. Cities also maintain an expensive fleet of buses and subway cars to ease the congestion created by the city's refusal to impose tolls. Some of the tab for this excess of travel on public transit is picked up by property taxpayers in the city. Some of that cost gets passed back in the cost of goods and services suburbanites consume while at work downtown. There are no free lunches. By hiding the true cost of the meal, what you get are smorgasbords that no one would want had they anticipated the price.

Problems Are Good for Business

One of the reasons for having government is to prevent excesses such as those on city streets. Instead of calming our feeding frenzy, city and provincial governments have set themselves up as brokers of excess. They are the middlemen who collect wealth and power by taxing us and providing us with services. Anything that increases the size of government increases the brokerage fee to politicians and bureaucrats. Government has been shrinking recently due to the pressure of debt, but where politicians can get away with keeping government big they do. The best way for a politician to ensure a large demand for his services is to hide the cost of those services. Unpriced roads lead to endless demand for roads. This guarantees a demand for the services of a public sector that owns and operates city streets and expressways.

Keeping roads unpriced also leads to congestion. Instead of solving the congestion with a toll, governments conclude that more intervention is needed, in the form of government-run buses and subways. The result is more business for our leaders. A.A. Hooker summed up this tendency in his 1939 assessment of the international grain trade,

"The attempts by governments to regulate commerce both domestically and internationally have resulted in a series of mistakes, each one requiring some fresh legislation to counterbalance the initial blunder, until the maze of restriction on every form of industry has made clear thinking very difficult." In the case of city traffic, the maze of transit subsidies and unpriced roads makes it hard for voters to see a solution. The property and income taxes that subsidize roads and transit lobotomize voters. These taxes go into the general government pot and may be put to any use. In this climate, it is hard to tell whether you are getting value for your tax dollar and so it is difficult to complain to your leaders that taxes are too high.

User fees for roads would stop this nonsense. Fees would unplug roads and streets, and prevent politicians from leading us to a feast we would rather avoid. The horn honking behind me is a reminder that I have been at this intersection too long. Some notions are clear, but a question nags. Sure, let user fees rule. But which user fees? Who sets them? To get the answer I will let government subsidize my thoughts, as I cruise along the toll-free expressway.

Read On ...

"Transport Strategy the Free Market Way." *Transport*, March-April 1994, pp. 12-14.

Batchelor, Charles. "White paper will define public transport policy." *Financial Times of London* Survey. February 19, 1998, p. 1.

Boucher, Michel (1996). "Highway Costs and Revenues in Quebec: Evidence and Analysis." École nationale d'administration publique working paper #9604.

Cox, Wendell, and Jean Love. "How the Competitive Market Can Make Canadian Transit Efficient and Effective." In Filip Palda, ed. *Essays in Canadian Surface Transportation*. Vancouver: Fraser Institute, 1995, pp. 141-178.

Elliot, James R. (1997). "Cycles within the System: Metropolitanisation and Internal Migration in the US, 1965-90." *Urban Studies*, 34:21-41.

Keeler, Theodore, et al. *The Full Cost of Urban Transport*. Berkeley: Institute of Urban and Regional Development, Monograph No. 21, 1975.

Kraus, Marvin (1989). "The Welfare Gains from Pricing Road Congestion Using Automatic Vehicle Identification and On-Vehicle Meters." *Journal of Urban Economics*, 25:261-281.

Michie, R.C. (1996). "The International Trade in Food and the City of London Since 1850." *European Journal of Economic History*, 25: 369-404.

Mills, Edwin S. and Bruce W. Hamilton. *Urban Economics*, 4th ed. Boston: Scott, Foresman and Company, 1989.

Poole, Robert W. Jr. (1996). "Defederalizing Transportation Funding." Policy Study No. 216 (October), Reason Foundation.

Vickerey, William (1963). "Pricing in Urban and Suburban Transport." In Richard Arnott, ed. *Public Economics: Selected Papers by William Vickrey*. Cambridge: Cambridge University Press, 1994, pp. 307-319.

_____. "General and Specific Financing of Urban Services." In Richard Arnott, ed. *Public Economics: Selected Papers by William Vickrey*. Cambridge: Cambridge University Press, 1994, pp. 350-383.

three
PRIVATIZING
TRANSIT

The best fertilizer for land is the footprint of its owner.
—Lyndon Johnson

AT THIS HOUR, HONEST PEOPLE ARE IN BED. The roads belong to revellers, mischief makers, and one bold soul in search of the perfect user fee. If he had his way, this fee would reflect the true cost of providing the service and this true cost would be as low as possible. Where should our Percival of city finances look for his Holy Grail?

Percival could look to a king for guidance. Kings have a long tradition of setting user fees. Their way has been to license a subject who bids the highest fee to operate a turnpike. The subject is then free to maintain the road, ensure safe passage, charge a toll, and sell the route. The ability to reap these rewards leads the licensee to invest in his road's upkeep. This is how the right to property broadens people's perspective and leads them to take care of what they own.

Setting Limits to Property

However, the problem with this arrangement is that the property rights the King has sold are too broad to yield the ideal user fee. These rights include the exclusive right to operate the King's road. No one can build a rival road. The exclusive right to operate says that you own a part of the King's army. If anyone tries to compete with you, you can call on soldiers to scatter the competitors. Under a regime such as this one, you can bet that fares are going to reflect more than the good care the owner takes to maintain his investment. Fares will also reflect his ability to scare away competitors by thuggery.

There are few kings left today, but modern democracies have not abandoned the old ways. Governments still sell exclusive licenses to operate. These auctions usually encourage investment, but the prices charged to users are higher than the costs to operate the system. When prices are kept too far above cost, people consume less than when prices are close to cost. Frustrated consumption is a sign of the damage that an exclusive license or "monopoly" can inflict.

Protect Us from All Monopoly

To protect us from private monopolies, many governments have taken over direct operation of roads, transit, water, and other municipal services. The notion is that a government-run monopoly is less likely to gouge consumers with excessive user fees than a privately-run monopoly. Whether voters get a fair deal out of government ownership depends on how the owner is steering the ship. Public monopolies, by definition, have no shareholders to watch over costs and reap the benefits of high profits. The public monopoly has only "stakeholders." As it works out, some people end up holding the stake, while others get impaled by it. In their study of Air Canada, Berkeley economist David Gillen and University of British Columbia economists Tae Oum and Michael Tretheway suggest that the grabbers are the unionized workers and managers of the public corporation. By pushing for high salaries and easy workloads, employees push up the costs of the public corporation. To remain solvent the corporation meets these costs by charging monopoly prices or by getting a government subsidy. This is how the riches to be gained from a monopoly can be grabbed by stakeholders in a public corporation. The bewildered citizen, it seems, is not safe from having his wallet picked as long as someone has the power of monopoly.

Why Privatize?

Getting rid of monopolies brings us only part of the way to the right user fee. Another step is to choose whether government or the private sector should be providing the service. Economists Anthony Boardman and Aidan Vining studied the efficiency of 500 industries that included electric utilities, refuse, water, health-services, financial services, airlines, fire-services, and non-rail transit. They found that publicly-owned companies had significantly higher costs than private companies. Other studies showing the benefits of privatization fill the academic journals, though studies showing public companies are more efficient also exist, and so the cautious intelligent consumer might wish to look these over. A number that keeps coming up in studies of privatization is that it lowers costs by 30 percent. If this is a reliable ballpark figure, then 30 percent is the premium that citizens pay for letting public companies run city services.

Why should private companies be more efficient producers than public companies? A private company collects the fruits of its efforts in the form of cash profits. One way to keep profits high is to keep costs low. Shareholders insist on keeping costs low and have the power to make the company floor shake by voting out poor managers. Managers also live in fear that shareholders will sell their stock to a "corporate raider." Raiders specialize in spotting poorly-managed companies whose potential is neglected. They buy out the company, put sleepy-eyed managers to the oar, and sell off the fleet of executive jets.

In a public corporation there are no shareholders to collect the benefits of efficient operation. There are only stakeholders who try to take,
in whatever form they can, what the company earns. Workers and
managers get their hands on these earnings by increasing costs. High
salaries, not bothering to innovate, and loafing are means by which
these stakeholders grab the public corporation's earnings. Politicians
have some incentive to keep down these depredations. But politicians are protected from voter wrath by a four-year guarantee of
power. If executives at IBM had a similar guarantee we would see the
costs of this company multiply like a computer virus. The weak link
between citizens and their public corporation and the fact that profits
go to the government treasury instead of shareholders combine to
make the public corporation a powerhouse of inefficiency.

A private company keeps costs low partly by investing in research
and infrastructure. Private companies invest in these activities because shareholders are able to cash in on the benefits. Critics of privatization claim that private companies will skimp on investments that
produce quality service. Supporters of privatization answer by point-
ing to the crumbling public houses of Cabrini Green in Chicago or the
potholed streets of Montreal. Neither side gets the point.

Private entrepreneurs may produce more or less quality than the public sector. They may invest less or they may invest more. None of this
is important. What matters is whether the private sector is investing
the *right* amount at the right cost. Companies have an incentive to
keep investing up to the critical point where the amount that consumers are willing to pay for the improvement is what it costs the
company to make the improvement. If a public company pays too little for its labour and machines, as is usually the case in countries
where dictators enslave their people, then we might expect to see
overinvestment. If the managers and unions of the public company
get little or none of the profits from improving service, we can expect
to see too little investment.

Nothing says government companies cannot fine-tune their investments and the quality of their services as effectively as private companies. But things work out differently. Political forces pull governments either to invest too much or too little. To fine-tune your investments to the right point, you need to keep in mind the consumers who will be using the system and the workers and investors who provide the service. Politicians and public employees have less incentive to keep the consumer in mind than the private entrepreneur. Their incentives are weaker because, as I suggested earlier, the profits from investments do not go directly into the pockets of politicians and public sector workers. Politicians try to get their gains from the infrastructure by impressing voters with fancy projects and hiding the cost through debt financing. Sometimes public employees manage to pressure leaders for higher salaries. Such a squeeze on the treasury may leave little for the upkeep of infrastructure. The flow of public investment can be diverted by such forces.

A Tale of Two Subways

A sense of the price of quality comes from the lives of Charles Tyson Yerkes and Nikita Sergeievich Khrushchev. Yerkes was a 19th-century financier and stock promoter. Khrushchev became a star in the Russian communist firmament in the 1930s as a commissar for public works. I doubt they met, but if they had, over a cocktail at the Hotel Ukraine in Moscow or at Boodles in London, the talk would have turned to the subways on which each man built his name. At the turn of the century, 63-year-old Yerkes came from Chicago to London in the company of his 23-year-old girlfriend (they called them mistresses in those days). He gathered investors to help buy out most of London's subway lines and to raise funds for new deep-level lines. He electrified the subway and powered it by building Europe's' biggest electric plant. When Yerkes died a few years later, his company, Underground Electric Railways of London, spanned London with the world's most advanced subway system. The stock market was impressed enough to value his system at fifty million pounds. This value reflected years of thought, negotiation, initiative, and sweat. Yerkes had countless conversations with investors from whom he raised money. During these conversations he explained his views and was forced to consider the views of others. Workers had to be persuaded by salaries that compensated them for the risks of deep-level work. The 50 million pounds also reflected the willingness of consumers to pay for an unsubsidized service.

Khrushchev would have marvelled at such patience. "My poor capitalist friend!" I can see Khrushchev exclaiming as he spills his drink on Yerkes' shoe, "didn't all this explaining and sweet talking drive you mad? When I was building the Moscow subway I only consulted engineers and my boss Kaganovich. For the most part, I ignored them! I remember my chief engineer Stepanov coming to me with some sob story about buildings collapsing along the line of excavation because we had not shored them up. So I tell him, 'What's the matter with you? Are you frightened of buildings?' You see, Charles Tyson, during the construction of the underground we knew, of course, that we were tunnelling under a great city, that every disturbance of existing foundations might lead to disaster; nevertheless, during the first period of construction we did not show particular vigilance. We tunnelled at four times the rate recommended by experts. I lengthened shifts and made workers serve as many as five consecutive shifts on duty. I gave workers in the underground caissons shifts of ten or eleven hours in spite of the fact that four hours was considered dangerous to human life, due of course to the fact that we had to maintain the air pressure at 2.4 atmospheres to contain silt. Nobody knows how many died as a consequence of catastrophes and depth sickness. That much is true. But they were for the most part volunteers. Our Cheka of course was active in rooting out saboteurs and inspiring workers with their cleansing zeal. The result? No one dares question it. My subway is worth more than yours. It cost the Soviet people 350 million rubles to build that first stretch in 1934.

More than the 300 million rubles spent that year on the production of consumer goods for the whole country. Our subway contains more marble than all the Tsarist palaces combined. Granite, bronze, and porphyry are everywhere you look. What more could you ask for?"

The verdict of historians is that a great deal less could have been asked for. The Moscow subway was an extravagance bought at a price in lives and money that would have made capitalists blanch. It was built on the backs of cheap labour to aggrandize Khrushchev and Stalin. The investment in Moscow transit came at too high a price because public managers had monopoly control of the resources that would advance their careers. They cashed in on this monopoly control by glorifying themselves at the expense of Russian consumers and workers. Yerkes had no such power. Nobody associates the London underground with bloodshed and extravagance. Yerkes built the underground by a consensus of investors who had their eye on costs and workers who had to be paid a fair wage. Such is the private way of balancing many concerns to pick a reasonable level of investment.

Price Controls Please

Talking about the benefits of privatization is not the same as reaping those benefits. Sometimes the utility being privatized is so large that once it lands on the market it will be the only producer and have no competitors. Such a monopoly will not share the benefits of its low costs with consumers unless government does something to keep prices down. Think of a city's network of streets. For a bus company to charge the lowest possible user fee in line with the true overall costs of running buses, it has to pay whoever operates city streets close to the true cost of building and maintaining those streets. Here is the third ingredient for setting the right user fees for transit services: the infrastructure on which that transit system runs has to be correctly priced. "Correct" once again means a price that reflects the lowest possible cost of providing infrastructure. But more than this, those who control the infrastructure have to be ready to write innovative contracts with transit operators. What this means we shall see in a moment. But first let us focus on prices.

There are two ways to control infrastructure prices. To see how each works let us go down to street level. The city has sold off all downtown streets to one private operator who will clear snow and make repairs. The city sells to a single operator because it gets a better price. If it sold each street to a different operator, thousands of entrepreneurs would have to knock heads and negotiate a way to run the city's network of streets. This added negotiating cost would lower the bidding amounts. The city allows the operator to charge a base rate that covers part of his maintenance costs. The city also allows him to set peak hour tolls just high enough to discourage traffic jams. Without such regulation, the operator would exploit his lease over the streets to charge too high a toll.

The problem with this sort of price control is that city bureaucrats have to know what it costs to maintain streets and tolls that allow a free flow of traffic. The civil servants who regulate private telephone monopolies have faced this problem for close to a hundred years. And for most of that time, telephone companies have bamboozled government with inflated estimates of what it costs to run their systems. Civil servants are lost in these proceedings because they do not have the knowledge of costs that results from years of running a business. Civil servants could save themselves the bother of having to watch over private sector monopolists. All they need do is encourage competition among private providers of city services. Competition is another word for price control. Only this time, the control does not come from civil servants. It comes from rival producers.

Rivals know the true cost of providing a service. To grab the market from each other, they reveal this true cost by offering the lowest possible price. Competition forces producers to share the fruits of their efficiency with consumers. Any producer who is selfish and charges too high a price loses his customers. Economist Evsey Domar explained this remarkable result of competition as follows: "The power exercised by consumers over producers requires no police, no compulsion, and no letters to the editor of *The New York Times*. It works silently, like gravity. All the consumer has to do is not come back to the store, not buy the same product ever again."

Mechanics of Price Control

How would consumers exercise power over the private owner of city streets? Every few years, citizens elect purchasing agents. These agents like to call themselves leaders and politicians. We can allow them this conceit, provided they do their jobs, which is to get us city services at the lowest cost. By banding together and delegating bargaining power to these purchasing agents, citizens can negotiate fair deals with providers. In the case of streets, the way to pick a provider is to give sole operation of the streets to the provider who offers the lowest bid. Bids open again in several years when technology has advanced enough for rivals to come up with lower bids. The trick is in setting the length of the franchise. Make it too brief and consumers will not have the time to judge the quality of the services. Make it too long and you protect the bidder from rivals who have discovered ways of providing the service at a lower cost. Picking the right length of time produces a monopoly without fangs. This is how you introduce competition and consumer control into businesses where there can be only one provider at a time.

London Calling

England is an example of a country that got some of the ingredients of transit user fees right, and made mistakes with other ingredients. In 1985 London defanged its public bus monopoly and allowed private companies to run exclusive services over half the city. To win a route, a company bids against rivals. The lowest bid wins. The city collects all the money from bus rides and pays the bus line the amount of its bid. Between 1985 and 1996 the real cost per kilometre of running buses in London fell by 45.7 percent. In Canada, where governments have protected our innocence from privatization of buses, real transit vehicle operating costs per kilometre rose by an average of 36 percent between 1970 and 1990.

Costs fell in London's case because rivals were forced to compete for bus lines. Unfortunately, London forgot the second half of the recipe for competition, which is to give consumers an immediate share of the benefits through lower prices. The city still controls fares and it-self pockets most of the savings from bus operation. Of course some-one benefits from these savings, perhaps a public sector union or a politician refurbishing his office. To the people who ride the buses the benefit is less clear.

Government-mandated competition is fine for the extreme case in which a market can hold only one producer at a time. This extreme is rarer than our leaders are likely to admit. Government-mandated competition is appealing to politicians because it creates a demand for their services. They are the middlemen who take the bids and de-cide whether the suppliers give quality for service. A basic principle of business, and life, is to leave middlemen at the bus stop whenever possible. There is no reason why buses should be regulated in this manner. It is possible to have several companies serving the same street. Under such competition, riders benefit immediately from competition, without paying politicians to oversee transit.

Bring Back the Jitney

The benefits from competition by private providers of transit do not come only in the form of lower prices. Benefits also come from inno-vations in service. No Canadian under the age of 80 will remember hail-and-ride buses, also known as jitneys. In 1915 the jitney ap-peared in Los Angeles. That same year it appeared in Vancouver. Two years later even middle-sized towns such as Belleville, Ontario had jitney companies. The jitney filled a gap left by regular buses. The jitney did not run as regularly as the bus, but for travellers who did not care about precision, the jitney compensated by being flexible. It picked you up where you stood and dropped you off where you asked it to. Workers for the traditional bus and streetcar monopolies felt threatened by such audacity. They put pressure on governments to outlaw the jitney and by 1930 nearly all Canadian cities had wiped it out. If we allowed competition back into public transit, we would see the return of innovations such as the jitney and the invention of services which are hard to imagine, such as buses on which a security guard rides and luxury commuter buses with meal service, short movies, and perhaps even poetry readings.

Dependence of Privatization on User Fees

The only condition for a happy outcome to this free-for-all in transit competition I am proposing is that the pricing of city streets reflect the lowest possible costs of operating streets. As I explained earlier, unpriced streets are open to abuse. Drivers on their way to the suburbs are not the only potential culprits. If we allow buses to compete, we may get a surplus of buses clogging the streets. This is what seems to have happened in parts of Britain outside of London where bus competition was allowed but streets were not priced.

London's experiment in privatization seems to have worked better because politicians controlled the number of buses by allocating temporary monopolies to a limited number of operators. If streets were priced and run by private operators, there would be no need for politicians to determine who can run a bus. Prices that prevent congestion reflect the will of those who value the service most. If bus lines are not able to keep down costs and if there is little demand for service, prices will send a clear message: get off the street; others value using it more for their vehicles than you as the bus operator do. Sifting through the people who value a service from those who value it less is what prices are about.

Giving a company a long-term contract to manage streets provides more than low street tolls. Such an arrangement also turns streets into safe havens for innovators. Take the tragic case of Super Shuttle in Los Angeles. The story starts out well. Super Shuttle rose to prominence in the 1980s as an alternative to buses and taxis. The company hired drivers who knew how to get around Los Angeles and gave them excellent vans to drive. It built a reputation for fast, efficient service, especially at airports.

SuperShuttle was driven out of business by "interlopers" who knew where Super Shuttle customers gathered at airports. These hit-and-run artists were rude, drove rickety machines, and knew little about how to get where the customer wanted to go. The only advantage was that they offered a lower price than Super Shuttle. These interlopers exploited Super Shuttle's name and got away with it because many of their customers would never pass through LA again.

A study by Washington's Brookings Institution argues that had Super Shuttle been able to buy "curb rights," things might have turned out differently. A curb right gives you the exclusive right to pick up customers where they expect you. Your name gets tied to a location. How much you pay for the curb right depends on how much value you can bring to customers waiting at that curb. Your bid would depend on long-term returns because the right would encourage you to do your utmost to attract clients by building a solid reputation.

This may seem like a strange way of looking at streets, but it is little different from the way we look at the vineyards of Chateauneuf-du-Pape in France. These wines are produced from more than just good soil. They flow from the expertise of local winemakers who have worked for generations to figure out how to use the grape. That local knowledge is important is obvious to any amateur winemaker who has ordered grapes from the area only to produce low-grade swill in his basement. Imagine what would happen now if this basement vintner were allowed to market his wine as coming from Chateauneuf-du-Pape. The brand-name's value would plummet. The reduced profits would discourage vintners in the Chateauneuf-du-Pape region from tending their vines.

Some curb rights show up in the parking crescents of downtown hotels. A taxi company will pay the hotel a fee for the exclusive right to park its cabs in the crescent. Anyone who has taken these cabs will know that their quality is usually better than that of the cabs you flag down. Better cab companies can bid more for curb rights because they can count on a more devoted clientele than the gypsy cabs you hail from the sidewalk. The benefits of maintaining a good reputation encourage these companies to keep their cabs clean and their service efficient. Imagine how much more service we would get from a competitive transit system where street curbs are open for auction to buses, taxis, and vans. At present we have only our imaginations to rely on. Cities keep the curbside monopoly for their buses and discourage all other innovators.

Subsidies and Inefficiency

Sooner or later, some countries will catch on to the benefits of pricing their roads. When the idea dawns, these nations will be poised to outcompete their neighbours. Not only will they have cleared their streets and encouraged their citizens to choose the least expensive way to get about, they will also have rid themselves of the need to subsidize transit.

Today to keep transit running, cities have to dish out subsidies that would have made a pyramid-building Pharaoh blush. On average in Canada only 55 percent of transit operating costs are recovered through fare box revenues. The shortfall in revenue comes in part from property taxes. In 1996, Toronto property owners paid $104 million to subsidize the fares of the Toronto Transit Commission. The urban transit Moloch feeds with similar appetite in Montreal, Vancouver, and Edmonton.

Where property taxes fall short, provincial subsidies rush in. In transit, as in other municipal services, provincial governments grant money for buying new hardware and covering daily operating costs. In Ontario the province pays 75 percent of rapid transit construction costs and 75 percent of the cost of buying and repairing buses, garages, and transit terminals. Provincial subsidies for the costs of daily operation vary between 16 percent and 25 percent. These subsidies added up to $760 million dollars in 1996. Fortunately for the citizens of Ontario, the provincial government decided to phase out most of these subsidies starting in late 1998 and allow municipalities to raise the shortfall through transit user fees. Ontario's bold move will be complete if and when it allows municipalities to charge for city road use. In the US in the 1980s the federal government helped to finance more than $20 billion of construction on new urban rail systems in 14 cities. The cost of servicing riders of these expanded systems makes eyes pop. Per passenger costs on Los Angeles' new commuter rail system may reach as much as $30,000 every year.

Provinces also subsidize each others' transit. In the 1970s and 1980s, Ontario's Urban Transit Development Corporation (UTDC) got into the business of making and selling light rapid trains for urban transit. Before going bankrupt and dragging half a billion dollars of taxpayer money to Hades, UTDC sold one of its train systems to Vancouver. When Vancouverites ride their SkyTrain, they are travelling on a cushion of lost Ontario tax dollars, above the reality of costs.

Subsidies not only offend taxpayers, but they encourage transit service inefficiency. A study of public school bus systems by US economists Richard Silkman and Dennis Young found that subsidies from higher levels of government for local public school buses did not always increase the number of rides. In fact, every additional dollar of subsidy tended to increase costs by 47 cents. Public sector unions were using part of the subsidies to raise their salaries and relax on the job. None of this would happen if streets were priced, and transit was private.

When I think of subsidized transit and unpriced streets, it strikes me that we need a political Susan Powter to shout "Stop the Insanity!" Powter is a diet guru who has exposed the diet industry as a collection of confused scientists and frauds. Transport in the city has come to a similar state. To restore sanity we need to make users pay and we need fair prices. Fair prices will come from setting private providers in competition with each other. These are the keys to a city's prosperity. Let's flatten the obstacles that a century of subsidies and public ownership have put in the way of free movement.

As I pull into my driveway, it strikes me that transport is not the only city service in need of privatization and user fees. Water, police, garbage, and parks could do with the same sort of treatment. So what is nagging me? Am I forgetting something?

Read On....

Boardman, Anthony E. and Aidan R. Vining (1989). "Ownership and Performance in Competitive Environments: A Comparison of the Performance of Private, Mixed, and State-Owned Enterprises." *Journal of Law and Economics*, 32:1-33.

Bradshaw, Bill. "The Future for London's Bus Services." *Transport*, January-February 1994, pp. 16-18.

Cory, Denis C. (1985). "Congestion Costs and Quality-Adjusted User Fees: A Methodological Note." *Land Economics*, 61:452-455.

Crankshaw, Edward. *Khrushchev: A Career*. New York: The Viking Press, 1966.

Davis, Donald F. (1989). "Competition's Moment:; The Jitney-Bus and Corporate Capitalism in the Canadian City, 1914-29." *Urban History Review*, 18:103-122.

Domar, Evsey D. *Capitalism, Socialism, and Serfdom: Essays by Evsey D. Domar.* Cambridge: Cambridge University Press, 1989.

Gillen, David W., Tae Hoon Oum, and Michael W. Tretheway. "Privatization of Air Canada: Why it is Necessary in a Deregulated Environment." *Canadian Public Policy*, 15:285-299.

Gillingwater, David, Alan Bryman, and Iain McGuiness. "Survival Strategies in a Deregulated Bus Market." *Transport*, May-June 1994, pp. 20-21.

Gomez-Ibanez, Jose A. and John R. Meyer. *Going Private: The International Experience with Transport Privatization.* Washington D.C.: The Brookings Institution, 1993.

Klein, Daniel B., Adrian T. Moore, and Binyam Reja. *Curb Rights: A Foundation for Free Enterprise in Urban Transit.* Washington D.C.: The Brookings Institution, 1997.

MacGregor, John. "Transport Strategy—The Free Market Way." *Transport*, January-February 1994, pp. 12-14.

Silkman, Richard H. and Dennis R. Young. *Subsidizing Inefficiency: A Study of State Aid and Local Government Productivity.* New York: Praeger, 1985.

Tompson, William J. *Khrushchev: A Political Life.* London: MacMillan Press, 1995.

White, Peter. "The Future of Buses in London." *Transport*, November-December 1994, pp. 17-19.

four

THE SOUP
KITCHEN
CITY

It is your own interest that is at stake when your next
neighbour's wall is ablaze.
—Horace

WHERE ARE THE POOR IN THESE MUSINGS ABOUT THE GLORIES
of user fees and privatization? Free buses and subways, parks, libraries, water, police, fire protection, and road maintenance appear to
help the city dwellers with modest incomes. Wouldn't user fees hit
these people hardest? Isn't their protection an immovable pillar in
the defence of subsidized city services?

The problem with providing city services for free or below cost can be
grasped by riding the Toronto subway from its northern Finch station
down to the central stations of Bloor and Union, or in Montreal between Atwater and McGill. A glance reveals well-dressed yuppies
sipping cappuccino, reading the business pages on their way to work.
Further evidence of the problem comes to light in summer when
neighbours fill pools and hose lawns with unmetered water. Are

these really the people we want to be helping with free city services? If your answer is "No" then you have understood that free services help not only the poor but anyone else who uses them. Cities with free access to most services redistribute money like Caesar throwing coins from his chariot. Caesar could have saved himself money and the trouble of plundering nations, if he had thrown coins only to citizens in need.

Targeting Aid

Turning the city into a vast soup kitchen is no way to help the poor. The soup kitchen city turns off our brains, encourages excess, and leaves little for the poor. Earlier, I explained that user fees make us smart consumers and producers. Fees force us to think whether we really value getting on the subway enough to pay. If not, we will step aside to leave room for someone else on a more urgent mission. The restraint and thought that fees produce are lost when you turn the city into an open banquet table of public services. The property taxes we eventually pay do not moderate our consumption because they are not related to how much we "pig out." Frenzied feeding by the general public leaves few resources to help the poor.

Wouldn't it make more sense to put away the shotgun and solve this mosquito-sized problem with a swatter? Instead of taxing everyone and siphoning the money through a dense bureaucracy to subsidize everyone, government should focus on helping the poor. Department of Revenue employees who now work to finger their fellows for tax evasion could contribute greater value to society by identifying those in need.

Targeting aid may sound like a reasonable idea but it is heresy to those who support the notion that government services should be universal. Universality means that rich and poor get equal belly-room at the government trough. It is a notion that has brought us governments in the shape of giant churns. A churn is a device that stirs milk in circles. The government churn cycles tax dollars. Your taxes are high so that government can transfer the money back to you in the form of social security, unemployment insurance, and free education for your children.

No matter which economist you consult, the cost of churning is pretty scary. Every dollar government raises takes between $1.30 to $2.00 out of your pocket. How so? Well, there is the dollar itself that gets lifted from your wallet. But there is a second effect called a "deadweight loss." This loss comes about because the tax raises the price of the good being imposed and forces you to cut back on your consumption. Unlike the tax, which at least goes into the government's pocket, the deadweight loss goes to no one. It is a pure, unrecovered economic waste. This waste from the consumption you lose has a value which economists estimate at between thirty and a hundred cents per dollar of government revenue. This means that the soup kitchen city is a big-time killer of resources. Universal access to city services forces taxes higher than they would be if the poor were directly targeted. Part of this excess is siphoned back to the non-poor but a large part, 30 to 100 cents on the dollar, disappears, into nobody's pocket.

The Power of Charity

How should we target the poor? The first step is to decide what we mean by poor. Everyone has his opinion on this, which I don't mean to belittle. But two views dominate the public debate and these are the ones I want to discuss.

The first view is that poverty is relative. Statistics Canada and poverty groups around the world see this as the only way of thinking about poverty. If your income is too far below the national average, these groups consider you poor. It does not matter if everyone's income in the country doubles. So long as you keep your place in the national income line-up, you will be identified by these social activist witnesses as remaining poor. Your condition will not have changed. The beauty of this relative definition is that the poverty rate can become whatever you wish it to become. All you have to do is choose a measure of inequality that suits you. The poverty industry in Canada relies on definitions of inequality that place 15 percent of the population in the economic cellar. Such a bloated number and the way it is rigged guarantee that the caretakers of government money for the poor will always have lots of business.

A measure of poverty harder to finagle comes from calculating how much it costs to feed, clothe, house, and otherwise maintain a human being at a level that preserves his health. France and the Czech Republic use this more old-fashioned "absolute" measure of poverty to calculate who qualifies for social assistance. In 1993 a Parliamentary Committee toyed with the idea of producing such a measure for Canada but abandoned the attempt after poverty activists hooted with indignation. The only dissenter to measure poverty along these old-fashioned lines has been economist Chris Sarlo at the University of Nipissing. His measure excites passions and recriminations because once he has finished grinding the numbers he finds that only 3 percent of the Canadian population fall under the threshold that divides the poor from everyone else. Three percent makes poor business for career-seeking social activists.

The poverty measure used determines the resources that a city, based on user fees, needs to devote to helping the poor. No matter which measure you choose, the form that aid should take does not vary. To protect the poor from the shift away from the soup kitchen city towards a user fee city, government can give them a rebate. This is how Ottawa introduced its value-added tax in the early 1990s. To shield the poor, Ottawa gave them a lump sum payment every year. This payment was calculated to keep their level of well-being the same after the tax as before it.

The trick to determining the amount of the rebat lies in knowing something about consumer budgets and preferences. If the price of transit doubles from $2 to $4 the poor consumer who takes 100 trips a year can be left just as well off as before by giving him a cash rebate of less than $200 (the two dollar price hike multiplied by 100 trips). The rebate is lower than we would imagine at first glance, provided the consumer can find substitutes for transit. Finding a friend to drive him for $2 a trip would be a perfect substitute and no rebate would be needed. Without such a friend, the best substitute might be a used bicycle selling for $100, capable of 50 trips for one year. The final cost to him now of 100 trips equals the $100 cost of 50 bicycle trips and the $200 cost of 50 transit trips. Spending $300 leaves him as well off as before the price hike. The $100 rebate plus the change to a different mode of transport cost less than the $400 it would cost to continue travelling in the old way at the new prices. Economists cannot measure the exact rebate but they have methods that let them come close.

The practice of rebates is now fairly well-established. When Ottawa introduced the goods and services tax in 1991 it scooped back 15 percent of revenues for rebates to the poor. In spite of this successful program's example, rebates for city user fees will irk social activists who believe that the poor should have minimal control over the aid they get. Such activists helped establish the US food stamp program and public housing. Their view was that the poor would neglect food and shelter and use the government money at the racetrack and/or the liquor store. To protect the poor from themselves, government force fed them "merit goods" such as food and other necessities.

User fees with a rebate are more likely to appeal to those who do not believe grownups, rich or poor, need a bureaucrat in nanny's uniform to put a spoon in their mouths. They will be attracted by the notion that the rebate protects the poor against the belt-tightening effects of user fees but does not numb them to the message that fees send.

Who will pay for the rebate? In a city financed largely by user fees, government coffers have little to spare for subsidies. Voluntary contributions could pick up the slack. If this sounds absurd, blame old habits. We have lived so long bent under the yoke of the taxman that we have trouble raising our necks to consider alternative methods of aiding to the poor.

Blame also the government's near monopoly on charity. Since the 1950s government has crowded private giving out of hospitals, schools, libraries, parks, and social assistance. The muscle used for this crowding comes from the tax collector. His depredations left charitably-inclined Canadians with little to donate. What works in one direction can also work in reverse. If government moves out of the charity business and lowers taxes, private citizens will pick up the slack. Evidence on this point is scarce but tantalizing. University of Iowa economist Stephen Ziliak studied the city of Indianapolis in the late 1800s. He found that when the city government cut back on welfare spending, private contributions to welfare filled the gap nearly dollar for dollar.

Few in Canada will remember, but up until the First World War, private charities took care of medical services, social welfare, and orphanages. Protestant and Catholic organizations, such as the Salvation army and St. Vincent de Paul Society, led these efforts but immigrant communities also formed their own protection societies. More recently, Canadians have shown impressive support for charities and philanthropic activities. According to a study by Duncan Campbell, Canada's charitable sector numbered 66,000 organizations in 1990, with recorded revenues of $39.7 billion and volunteer labour valued at $14.6 billion. That's 8.1 percent of national income. It is also about a quarter of what the federal government spends on services and interest and about a third of what it spends excluding interest. This figure is probably a low estimate of charity in Canada, as it does not include the revenues of non-profit organizations that are not registered charities, nor does it include the value of volunteer labour. The assets of these charities amounted to $54.6 billion with $7.4 billion in welfare, $15.4 billion in health, $15 billion in education, $14.2 billion in religion, $2.6 billion in community services. It seems that the will and organization exist to pick up any slack that city governments leave by bowing out of care for the poor.

Even if charities were not to contribute a cent to help the poor, we could count on the privatization dividend to cover the costs. As I mentioned earlier, when municipal governments change their suppliers, their costs go down. By switching from subsidized, unionized, public employees to private, competitive contractors, the city's costs may fall by as much as 30 percent. This windfall goes straight into the pockets of citizens who use the city's services. Out of these bulging pockets can come the charity necessary to compensate the 3 percent of the city's poor for the transition to user fees.

Libraries and Parks

Should children be made to pay for libraries and museums? Should everyone have to pay a dollar at the gate before entering a park? US industrialist Andrew Carnegie thought the answer was no. He sought matching funds from governments to help him build open libraries and parks. Walt Disney and his brother thought differently. Ambitious to become the world's biggest turnstile operators, they built the world's greatest parks. These examples tickle the imagination. If cities privatized their parks, citizens would get variety. Some parks would be open free of charge, courtesy of philanthropists. Others would charge a small fee and offer security patrols, supervision of children, and the staging of cultural events. Some parks owned by charities would rent space to restaurants. The Audubon Society has done something similar with its wildlife preserve in Texas. Most of the park is for wildlife, but a part is rented to oil explorers. The rent they pay maintains the wildlife.

History also teaches us that philanthropists and ordinary citizens will also come forth to fund libraries. Perhaps the only thing that would change if city governments bowed out of this activity is that libraries would charge corporate users, and subsidize citizens from the profits. Today public libraries give corporate users free access to their shelves. This is a bizarre use of tax money. Private philanthropies would not be so lax in choosing clients upon whom to bestow their favours. The same comments apply to museums.

Charity versus Compulsion

What if this faith in private sector charity proves misguided? Does this mean we should shy away from user fees? Hardly. If the private sector does not fill the gap, then the city can revert to arm-twisting. Arms should be twisted only as far back as required to help the needy adjust to user fees. Any further and you start sinking back into the mire of a city where no one moderates his consumption of public services.

Read On ...

Becker, Elisabeth and Cotton M. Lindsay (1994). "Does the Government Free Ride?" *Journal of Law and Economics*, 37:277-296.

Campbell, Duncan R. "The First General Map of Canada's Third Sector." School of Policy Studies, Queen's University, working paper 94-03, 1994. Platt, D.C.M. (1983). "Financing the Expansion of Cities, 1860-1914." *Urban History Review*, 11:61-66.

Dahlby, Bev G. and Giuseppe C. Ruggeri (1996). "The Marginal Cost of Redistribution: Comment." *Public Finance Quarterly*, 24: 44-62.

Palda, Filip (1997). "Fiscal Churning and Political Efficiency." *Kyklos*, 50:189-206.

Sarlo, Christopher A. *Poverty in Canada, Second edition*. Vancouver: Fraser Institute, 1996.

Usher, Dan (1986). "Tax Evasion and the Marginal Cost of Public Funds." *Economic Inquiry,* 24:563-86.

Ziliak, Stephen T. (1996). "The End of Welfare and the Contradiction of Compassion." *The Independent Review,* 1:55-73.

five
GREEN
FEES

He that hath no rule over his own spirit is like a city
that is broken down and without walls.
—*Proverbs*, Chapter 25, verse 28

Back home after a long evening of driving and ruminating, I
feel like taking a shower. Like most Canadians I have no hesitation
about letting the water flow. I live in one of the 55 percent of communities where water is not metered. I pay a fixed sum to the local utility, after which I can let the tap run all day, allow the toilet commode
to leak, drain my pool at will, hose the lawn, water the car.... Is there
no end to my bliss?

User Fees and Restraint

Canada's love affair with the open tap would amaze Europeans. The
average Canadian uses 350 litres of water a day. The British use 200
litres. The French get along with 150 litres a day. There are two inter-
twined reasons for this difference. First, Canadian communities are

more spread out than European ones. The broad lawns of a Toronto suburb would be a thing of fantasy in Paris and London. Second, in Canada 71 percent of rate schedules provide users no incentive to go easy on water. In France 95 percent of the population pays the full cost of the water it uses, as it uses the water. Urban sprawl and low water rates are related. A major attraction of suburban life is your own front and back lawn and swimming pool. Unmetered water makes this attraction affordable. For the sake of fairness, I should mention the US. The average American uses 425 litres a day.

Finding ourselves lower on the water gluttony scale than the US is no consolation. Environment Canada estimates that we could reduce our water use by 40 percent and hardly feel it. The amount we waste is a paradox. Canadians are not destructive people. Surveys show that we care about nature. "Recycling," "conservation," and "sustainable development" are among the first words that children learn (after "Nintendo"). In the 1980s, Canada resisted plans to build an aqueduct between British Columbia and California for fear of depleting our natural treasure of fresh water. But for all these fine sentiments, we behave with about as much care for water as the captain of the Exxon Valdez.

Most municipal governments have resisted charging citizens directly for water and waste water management. The charges that are levied cover only 65 percent of the true cost. The balance comes from lot levies, transfers from higher levels of government, cross-subsidies from charges on business users, and municipal debt. Even part of the 65 percent of costs that we do pay comes in a charge that imposes no restraint: the flat rate. There is no mystery to the Canadian who speaks of his concern for nature while he is busy abusing it. Talk is cheap, courtesy of municipal subsidies.

To what extent would user fees calm the compulsive toilet flusher and the Amazonian irrigator of lawns? In their study of Denton, Texas for the summer months between 1981 and 1985, economists

Julie Hewitt and Michael Hanemann found that for every ten percent increase in water prices, demand fell by 16 percent, after taking into account all other factors that might influence demand.

Here in Canada, those with meters use on average 40 percent less water than their fellows who pay a flat rate. As economist Harry Kitchen explains, "In part, this decline is psychological, but, in part, it is an economic response as consumers optimize their consumption once volume based rates are introduced. The usual pattern is for water use to fall substantially immediately following meter installation and then, to rebound somewhat as consumers become more familiar with the pricing scheme ... unmetered customers have no incentive to use water efficiently because the per unit price is zero." A report for Environment Canada's technology office points out that "It is far more cost-effective to conserve existing water resources to meet increasing demand for water, than to increase supply through expensive new infrastructure developments."

The Meaning of Efficiency

What does efficiency in water use mean? As with roads, or any other scarce city commodity, efficiency is the quest to provide a service to those who value it most by the those who can produce it at least cost. Water metering goes half way towards this ideal of efficiency. The price of water makes you think twice before washing the car. Is it really dirty or could it go a full week without a hose down? The more urgent is your neighbour's need for keeping his five children washed, the less inclined you will be to spray your car. Other people's urgent needs drive up the price. You will respond by turning down the tap.

Water gets used inefficiently when a government subsidy hides the true cost. As mentioned earlier, about 35 percent of the true cost of water is hidden from city dwellers. The truth we don't see encourages us to use water to a point where the benefit we get is lower than the true cost. Carrying on with projects whose costs exceed the benefits destroys wealth. This means that efficiency is not a zero-sum game. Getting rid of an economic inefficiency may improve everyone's lot.

To see this, consider that if I value a litre of water at one dollar per 1,000 litres but the cost of bringing it to me is two dollars, someone else is being shafted out of a dollar. Government may provide the shafting service by taxing consumption of food. How much would the person being shafted be willing to compensate the recipient of the water subsidy? The answer is that the shaftee is willing to pay the shafter more than a dollar to end the subsidy in return for having the tax revoked. He feels this way because a dollar of tax does him more than a dollar's worth of harm. First off, he loses a dollar, but the tax also raises the price of the good and forces the consumer to cut back on something he enjoys.

The lost pleasure from consuming less is what economists call a deadweight loss. Canadian economists have estimated this loss at somewhere between 30 cents and 80 cents per dollar of tax. Taking the low estimate, this means that the person being taxed is willing to pay the subsidized user of water up to 29 cents per hundred litres to get him to give up his water subsidy. The taxpayer would be ahead by one cent, and the subsidized user would be ahead by 29 cents. It is in this sense that water subsidies are inefficient.

For those who care about fairness, free or subsidized water also has hidden costs that allow heavy users of water to pay for their indulgence at the expense of light users. The heavy users may be rich, the light users poor. No one can tell whether justice is being served in a world where particular services are financed out of a general pot. All we know is that resources are being wasted.

Public Ownership and Costs

The other half of efficiency is making sure that the price recorded by the water meter reflects the cost of the most efficient way of delivering water. Some communities in Canada claim to charge full cost, but for the most part, this is a fib. As Harry Kitchen writes, "in almost all municipalities, water utilities, commissions, or departments seldom include all relevant operating costs in setting price ... depreciation costs are seldom included ... failure to incorporate depreciation means that the annual cost of the capital resources used up in the delivery of water services is not being captured in price.... As long as some operating costs are ignored ... it may be folly to comment on the efficiency of existing volumetric pricing structures."

Kitchen is saying that governments hide the true price of water with subsidies. This does not mean that getting rid of subsidies will give us efficient prices. Remember the definition: part of efficiency is producing a service at the lowest possible cost. Could water be supplied in Canada at lower cost? Local evidence is scarce because almost all water in Canada is supplied by government agencies. There are some differences among these agencies that give clues to how the cost of water could be lowered. Economist Harry Kitchen found that "municipalities supplying water through a utilities commission incurred significantly higher costs per-unit operating costs than did those municipalities where this service was administered and provided through a municipal department at city hall ... the main factors generating higher costs under a separate commission seem to result from weaker public accountability ... furthermore, the cost differential is not the result of a higher quality of service from commissions since service levels in all municipalities tend to be standardized."

Private Ownership and Costs

Kitchen's study hints that if private companies compete with each other to provide water, costs will fall. Private companies are accountable to shareholders interested in keeping costs down. Competition is a form of self-enforcing regulation. Any company that charges too much gets undercut by its rival. Evidence on the efficiency of private provision comes from the US. In a 1978 study of 112 US water utilities, economists Walter Crain and Chaim Zardookhi found that when government handed management of water to private firms, output per employee jumped by 25 percent. Public firms also used 65 percent more hardware to do the same job as private firms. Today in the US, privately-managed firms supply 20 percent of drinking water and 2 percent of waste water management.

In Canada, private providers of water are about as rare as the Coelacanth fish. It was not until the mid-1990s that a company called Dominion Waterworks was allowed to begin construction of Ontario's first privately-financed water and sewage treatment plant. The plant will serve the community of Rockland, population 6,800. The government of British Columbia discourages communities from turning to the private sector for their water. The largest private utility in the province is Whiterock Utilities Ltd. It supplies 3,000 customers. In 1996 the city of Montreal floated the idea of privatizing its water system. The idea sank after a torpedo attack by unions and big government activists.

Infrastructure Meltdown: Call the Private Sector!

Governments need to clear up their allergies to user fees and private sector producers. The Federation of Canadian Municipalities estimated that in 1985 between 15 and 40 percent of water infrastructure needed upgrading and repair and that the bill could run to $7.5 billion. The technology and transfer office of Environment Canada writes that "inadequate capital funding for aging distribution and collection systems has led to continuing loss of water supply through pipe leakage. It is estimated that leakage accounts for 12 percent of total municipal water use." In Toronto 28 percent of the volume sewers carry and plants treat is clean water from this kind of leak. Governments have shown themselves to be poor caretakers of the water infrastructure. And they admit that they do not have the money to fix that infrastructure properly. Soon they will have no choice but to turn to the private sector for investment help and to user fees to moderate demand.

To get a sense of how the private sector can help rebuild infrastructures, consider the case of the UK. By the late 1980s the UK's ten public water authorities were $8.5 billion dollars in debt and sitting on piles of deteriorating infrastructure. In 1989 the Thatcher government changed all of this by introducing the *Water Act*. The Act led to the creation of private companies responsible for owning and operating water and sewage utilities, meeting government water quality standards, and financing and upgrading infrastructure. When these companies went private the initial public offering of shares brought in $12 billion. This wiped clear the debt these utilities inherited from government. Companies were also given the right to charge for their services. Even though this charge is of the most stupid sort—a levy on property values—the money collected allowed the utilities to spend triple what governments used to spend on infrastructure. The result is (surprise!) that water quality has improved. In 1986 23 percent of sewage plants were discharging effluent. By 1991 this percentage had fallen to 6 percent. By the year 2000, companies will have built over 120 pesticide treatment plants, upgraded over 70 water treatment plants, and renovated 8 percent (25,000 kilometres) of water distribution mains. I could go on, but the picture is clear.

Call the Professionals

In part, the British managed this upgrade with the help of the French. Wine, gothic cathedrals, modern algebra, and the Chanel suit are among France's contributions to humanity. So is the science of water engineering. Two French firms bestride the water utility world like colossi: Générale-des-Eaux, founded in 1853, and Lyonnaise-des-Eaux-Dumez. In countries privatizing their water system, you will find both companies fighting it out for a piece of the action. They are the Microsofts of the water world. These companies have grown out of

France's policy of allowing private companies to underbid each other to supply citizens with water.

Competition takes many forms in France. At its purest the French grant a *concession* to the private company. The municipality specifies the kinds of water services it wants for its citizens, then solicits bids from private companies. The firm with the lowest bid gets to design, build, finance, maintain, and run the water facility for between 20 and 30 years. Customers pay the firm directly and the community renegotiates prices regularly to reflect taxes, inflation, and other surprises in the economy. A less purely private contract called an *affermage* divides the chore of supplying water. Under *affermage* the municipality builds new utilities but allows the private sector to operate them and collect fees. In France 95 percent of citizens have meters and the prices they pay reflect the true costs of providing the service. Out of this hothouse of competition came Générale-des-Eaux and Lyonnaise-des-Eaux. France's policy of letting only the strong survive has made it the world leader in water technology. They are owners or part-owners of private water concerns in the UK, US, and the Far East, and lead the way in research and development. Competition from the French has in turn spurred the British water firms to contest the French in the world market.

Uncharted Waters

Canada remains remote from international water expertise, like Japan before the arrival of Commodore Perry. Blame our isolation on the water shoguns. Canada's water industry is divided into thousands of fiefdoms ruled by local utilities and commissions. All is at peace in this land, as it has been for generations. A Quebec utility that is more efficient than an Ontario utility may not displace its Ontario neighbour by offering its subjects a better deal. Peace is good for managers, and it is good for union members—the samurai of this market.

Competition at home would force unions to take each other on in a bid to satisfy the lowly consumer-serf. Opening our doors to international expertise would lead to all-out war and an end to the traditional life of the water-samurai. Our isolation from competition is unfortunate for consumers, but above all, for producers and workers with pluck. The Technology Transfer Office of Environment Canada points out that government thwarts the private sector in most areas of the water business. Private companies are allowed a place in the manufacture of specialty equipment, construction, and consulting design. But the public sector keeps a grip on operating, financing, R & D, and part of construction. Even within this tiny field of activity, Environment Canada notes that "Canadian companies have developed an impressive range of internationally recognized high quality products and services in niche areas of water and waste water treatment."

We are left to wonder what opportunities Canada misses by stunting domestic competition. By the turn of the century the international market for water utilities and infrastructure will reach $60 billion. Canadian cities are nurseries in which our entrepreneurs could "learn the ropes" (or in this care "the pipes"). The speed at which they learn would accelerate if we allowed the French and British to compete on Canadian soil. Experience in other countries suggests that the French and British would contribute their international expertise and seek out Canadian partners with local expertise. Out of the mix, a dynamic Canadian water industry would be born, just as a dynamic Japan was born after it put its shoguns in business suits.

Why Britannia Doesn't Rule the Waves

Are there any examples of privatization and user fees in the world that should make city dwellers hesitate before giving up their subsidized, government-provided water? Surveys suggest that the British public is not amused by Westminster's privatization of the water system. It is easy to see why. With privatization, government subsidies shrivelled. The true cost of the resource became apparent. This always irks users. Worse still, user fees in the UK are of the very worst sort. Private utilities charge their clients based on the value of their property not of their water use. A citizen who wants to economize might as well not bother. Under such a system there is no payoff to closing the tap. The crowning insult to consumers is that the UK has not allowed its water utilities to compete. Westminster replaced a government monopoly that hid its costs under a blanket of subsidies by a private monopoly with a very tendency to gouge. The UK example shows that if you want consumers to get the full benefits of privatization you have to go all the way. Cry "privatize!" and let slip the dogs of competition.

Solid Waste: Nerves of Steel, Feet of Clay

In a 1985 study of 107 Canadian municipalities, University of Victoria economist James McDavid found that allowing the public sector to dispose of solid waste cost 51% more than when the matter was contracted out to the private sector.The annual collection cost per househould was on average $42.29 when the city collected garbage, and $28.02 when the task was contracted out to private firms. Were low private collection costs the result of shoddy service by the private sector? The answer was a resounding "no." Private sector operators use smaller crews than public sector operators, larger trucks, and dangle bigger carrots in front of their employees to get them to work efficiently. The result? Private sector employees collected on average 1.25 tones per hour whereas their public sector counterparts collected .64 tones per hour.

In 1996 McDavid and his colleague Karl Eder surveyed 327 local governments and asked them 60 questions intended to pinpoint why the cost of garbage collection differs from community to community. Using a conservative statistical technique likely to underestimate the savings from privatization, and after accounting for every conceivable factor that might influence the cost of collection, they found that private collection was on average $7.41 cheaper per household per year than the cost of public collection. Put in perspective, the most conservative savings estimate from privatization is a 12 percent drop in costs.

The boldness of local governments evaporates when it comes to making citizens pay directly for the garbage they produce. According to McDavid and Eder:

> Across Canada, 75 percent of all local governments reported using taxes alone as their way of paying for solid waste collection services. Of the remaining local governments, 22.6 percent reported charges to households as their way of paying for the service, but nearly all of these turn out to be periodic billings much like utility billings. A total of 29 local governments [in the survey of 327 governments] reported using prepaid tags as a way to raise revenue for all or part of their residential garbage collection, but only 3 reported using this system exclusively. The other 26 use it to charge for extra cans or bags above the limit specified for that local government.

The broader picture is that in 1993 local governments spent $1.4 billion on solid waste collection and disposal. Roughly half the cost is covered by businesses who pay solid waste tipping fees. In Ontario these tipping fees exceed the true cost of treating garbage. The excess helps to subsidize the garbage that ordinary citizens produce every week. Property taxes and subsidies from the province and Ottawa cover the remaining tab.

The Happy Polluter

Here again mystery shakes its rattle from the cave of Canada's conscience. How can such a responsible, nature-loving people dump crud on their lawns as if they were doing the universe a favour? In spite of recycling programs and anti-garbage public education, we are still in love with the trash bag. Blame local government's allergy to user fees for residential solid waste. This allergy costs us dearly.

Landfills are choking with trash. In the US the Environmental Protection Agency estimates that 80 percent of existing landfills will reach capacity in the next 20 years. Incinerators smudge the sky with fly ash and a toxic substance known as bottom ash. As economist Robin Jenkins writes, "The high value of land, the public's aversion to living near disposal sites and expensive new environmental regulations have all increased the cost of solid waste services." The power of user fees to solve the problem should not be ignored. Have you noticed those 25-cent boxes attached to supermarket shopping carts? Since supermarkets started this policy 20 years ago, I do not once remember leaving my cart stranded in the parking lot. There is no shopping cart "garbage" on parking lots because users pay a small fee to clean up their mess. The power of user fees to curb solid waste is just as significant. These fees can substitute for our conscience and make even the naughtiest polluter behave like a conservationist.

The example of shopping carts and 25 cents might not convince opponents of user fees for garbage. There is a surprising number of these people. They claim that user fees will not change behaviour. Such fees will only hurt the poor. Even if what they say is true, and it is not, user fees would still appeal to people because of their fairness. Studies of the US show that the rich put out the most garbage. They have bigger lawns and throw away more grass clippings than the poor. They buy more packaged goods. This is why garbage bags appear in profusion in front of mansions. We know about the difference in the garbage of the rich and poor because of the devoted work of economists Robert Richardson and Joseph Havlicek Jr.

These heroes of the profession analyzed waste they collected with their bare hands in 1972 from selected residential routes in Indianapolis. The routes were chosen to reflect a range of average household incomes. Richardson and Havlicek rolled up their sleeves and (yuk) separated the refuse into 11 different materials such as clear glass, aluminum, plastics, and grass. They found that aggregate waste and most individual wastes rose with household income. Their research raises the question of whether we want to live with a system where people who live to excess spread the cost of their gluttony to those who restrain themselves. A city in which everyone pays a flat rate for garbage encourages a perverse transfer of income from tidy citizens to polluters. The flat rate turns the city into an open field where garbage may be dumped at will. As with any common property problem, everyone shares the cost. Some receive more benefits than they pay for, others receive less. Gluttons win.

User Fees Swat the Litter Bug

Research by solid waste economists on the value of user fees is as solid as the wall of China: user fees reduce garbage. I will get to the anecdotes in a moment, but first the serious stuff. The studies that measure the effect of user fees on garbage disposal cover hundreds of municipalities with different levels of user fees. Researchers use a statistical technique known as regression to filter out the effects of other factors that might influence the amount of a community's garbage, such as the average income level of its residents, city density, weather, recycling costs, and the average age of the population.

Economist Robin Jenkins traced how residents in five US communities reacted to changes in charges for the volume of garbage they put out. She found that for every one percent increase in the user fee, the volume of garbage fell by slightly more than a tenth of a percent. She used these results to perform a thought experiment. What if a city that deducts the cost of garbage from property taxes switched to a user fee that covered the cost of collecting garbage? In the US, this would mean that for every 113-litre (32-gallon) container of refuse, the citizen would pay $1.31. In this scenario, waste would fall by 20 percent, which comes to half a pound per person, per day. The an-

nual quantity of waste put out by each person would fall by an average of 200 pounds. A city of 500,000 people would produce 47,800
fewer tons of garbage for landfills.

Seattle learned the benefits of user fees in the 1980s. In 1961 Seattle
founded the Solid Waste Utility, which recovered all its costs
through a flat annual charge. The city introduced modest user fees in
1981 and discovered that their effect on the garbage level was negligi-
ble. Then crisis struck. In the mid-1980s both the city's landfills had
to be closed after it was discovered they were threatening nature and
the health of residents. Seattle had to negotiate a quick deal with
neighbouring landfills on terms that were not favourable. To recover
this cost the Solid Waste Utility raised collection charges by 82 percent to $13.55 per month for the weekly collection of one 113-litre
container. What happened? Between 1981 and 1988 the average
number of garbage containers put out by single-family households
fell by 59 percent. From 1987 to 1988, residential waste going into
landfills fell by 10 percent. At around the same time, Perkasie, Penn-
sylvania replaced the flat annual $120 fee for residential garbage
pickup with a user fee. The switch was "revenue neutral," meaning
that user fees were not used to gouge citizens but rather to replace the
old flat tax. Between 1987 and 1988 Perkasie's waste dropped by 59
percent.

How do citizens manage to reduce their waste so much? In Perkasie
the amount recycled accounted for 28 percent of the reduction. The
remaining 31 percent can be accounted for largely by changes in consumer habits and separate collection of yard waste. A small part of
the drop was due to citizens burning and illegally dumping their
waste and to commercial users opting out of Perkasie's new system in
favour of a private waste hauler.

Consumers can change their habits by staying away from heavily-
packaged goods. The flat-fee system for garbage collection most communities use turns out to be a subsidy to consumers and to Kellogg,

Toblerone, and other wrap-artists. A citizen who does not have to pay for extra wrapping is getting a special discount for buying heavily-packaged goods. Part of this discount benefits him; another part goes into the manufacturers' pockets. By now you might have guessed: frugal citizens end up paying for this wastefulness. Once they become widespread, user fees will have their greatest impact on user habits. The national drop in demand for wrapping will force national manufacturers to think of less fluffy ways to market their products.

One point in this example stands out. User fees motivated some citizens to put their trash in commercial dumpsters under cover of night, or to burn it. How should the city handle this problem? Many communities force citizens to subscribe to a minimal level of garbage collection. I don't like the idea of forced anything, but I grant that the apostles of compulsion may have a point here. My view is that you should treat illegal garbage dumping like any other crime. Bag the culprit and dump him before the courts, instead of paying him not to misbehave. If cities cannot manage the feat, however, then perhaps imposing a minimal fee is in order.

Are user fees really to be credited with the miracle of reducing garbage piles? The problem with giving all the credit to user fees is that governments supplement fees with recycling programs and trash education programs. Separating the effect of fees from these other measures is like sorting a garbage pile into glass, paper, and remaining gunk. No doubt all these programs reinforce each other. If any idea stands as the leader in waste reduction it is user fees. As the OECD reported in its survey of the question, "studies conducted recently indicate consistent waste reduction in unit pricing communities in the US. For example, Dr. Daniel Blum of Duke University examined 14 cities with unit pricing schemes, and found an average 44 percent waste reduction, with a range of 18 to 65 percent reduction."

What Socialists Say

Perhaps the last word should belong to a study commissioned by the socialist government of Ontario in the early 1990s. In its 1993 report, Ontario's Fair Tax Commission wrote that "At present, municipalities cannot impose special levies for waste collection. The costs of collection must be recovered through general property tax revenues. As a result, there is little incentive either for individual taxpayers to reduce waste or for municipalities to provide higher-cost collection services to meet special needs.... Municipalities should be given the authority to charge for waste collection directly."

Sounds good to me. Now that everyone agrees, I can switch off the lights and get to sleep. I will ponder what to do about the city's police force when I wake.

Read On ...

Carr-Harris, Hugh. "Instruments Available to Waste Managers to Encourage Waste Minimisation." *Washington Waste Minimisation Workshop, Volume II, Which Policies, Which Tools?* Paris: Organisation for Economic Co-operation and Development, 1995, pp. 145-197.

Environment Canada. *Freshwater Series A-1 to A-6*. Environmental Citizenship Directorate, Ottawa, Ontario, 1992.

Hewitt, Julie A. and W. Michael Hanemann (1995). "A Discrete/Continuous Choice Approach to Residential Water Demand under Block Rate Pricing." *Land Economics*, 71:173-92.

Jenkins, Robin R. *The Economics of Solid Waste Reduction: The Impact of User Fees*. Aldershot: Edward Elgar, 1993.

Kitchen, Harry (1992). "Efficient Delivery of Local Government Services." Kingston: Industrial Relations Library, Discussion Paper No. 93-15.

McDavid, James C. (1985). "The Canadian Experience with Privatizing Residential Solid Waste Collection Services." *Public Administration Review*, pp. 602-608.

McDavid, James C. and Karl A. Eder (1997). *The Efficiency of Residential Solid Waste Collection Services in Canada: The National Survey Report.* Local Government Institute, School of Public Administration, University of Victoria.

McRae, James J. "Efficient Production of Solid Waste Services by Municipal Governments." Kingston: School of Policy Studies, Discussion Paper 94-11.

Richardson, Robert A. and Joseph R. Havlicek Jr. (1978). "Economic Analysis of the Composition of Household Solid Wastes." *Journal of Environmental Economics and Management*, 5:103-111.

Thompson Gow & Associates. *Canada's Untapped Resources: Public-Private Partnerships in Water Supply and Wastewater Treatment.* Ottawa, Technology Transfer Office, 1995.

VHB Research & Consulting Inc. *The Cost of Municipal Waste Management.* Ontario: Ministry of the Environment, 1993.

POLICE and FIRE

P OLICING IS THE ONE ASPECT OF GOVERNMENT SERVICE you might think should have nothing to do with privatization or user fees. Perhaps. The truth of the matter lies in asking ourselves what is special about the police that exempts it from competition and consumers' wishes. Police have a monopoly on force. This means they can exercise their power as they see fit, subject to the control of police boards, politicians, and somewhere down a very distant line, voters. Isn't this reason enough for the state to operate the police? Not really.

If you want to prevent the police from abusing their power, then you regulate the police. Does the need to stop companies from polluting justify government ownership of all businesses that pollute? Is the need to guarantee that food products are safe from disease a reason for government to own all farms and processing plants? The same applies to police. To control police abuses, you form a smaller police force to guard the guardians. This is not a flight of fancy. In the US, private police forces outnumber public police by 2 to 1. They arrest, patrol, protect, and investigate just like public police.

Private police forces fill the gap left by the public police. This should come as no surprise. Public police are a unionized organization, running along strict labour codes that discourage innovation and verve. In the early 1990s, the bungling and buck-passing of Ontario police in the case of the husband-and-wife team of killer-rapists are an example of the incompetence that breeds in enterprises where control is lax. Samples of body fluids that police left unanalyzed for years, eyewitnesses whose reports were ignored, and information from neighbouring police zones that was not investigated are just a few instances of police oversight that were summarized in an official review of the case.

Every organization has its problems and the police should not be singled out unfairly. But questions have to be asked of an organization (the police) that is protected from going out of business (subsidies raised through property taxes), where there is minimal feedback from consumers (victims and potential victims of crime), and where the people who finance the venture (taxpayers) have almost no say in how it is run.

Government's Role

If we accept that government should not own and operate the police, we have to ask to what extent government needs to regulate. Regulation of city police has to face up to two problems that the private market may not be able to deal with. The first problem is that police are licensed to use force. Force has no place in a private market, except to punish violations of explicit and implicit agreements. An explicit agreement is a contract two people hammer out. An implicit agreement is that private property and the human person are inviolable. By living in society you accept these terms without having to sign your name to them at the notary's office. If the police overstep the bounds of implicit and explicit agreements they interfere with the private market. Markets work by agreement. A corrupt policeman hired by a mustache-twirling capitalist can subvert the market and turn it into a dictatorship where force, rather than agreement, reigns. Here we need government to step in. If we can trust our politicians to control the use of force, we can delegate them the duty of policing the police. Politicians can do this by appointing police inspectors, just as government ensures building standards by appointing building inspectors.

Mandatory Police for Open Streets

The second reason government must intervene is that many areas of the city are public property. Access is available to everyone. No one is interested to finance the area's safety. This is the same sort of problem you get in health care. Hospitals are forced to accept anyone who comes in an emergency, whether he is insured or not. In this sense hospitals are public property. This explains why 30 percent of the US population does not bother to buy medical insurance. To protect hospitals against bankruptcy, government subsidizes this 30 percent slice of the population.

There are two ways to control this public property problem. The first is simply to convert public property into private property. Take as an example the private city of Irvine, California. 110,000 people live in "microvillages" governed by residents' associations. Woodbridge Village, which has 27,000 residents, advertises that "Here you don't just buy a house, you buy a lifestyle." Some villages are open. Anyone can drive through. Others are closed and do not admit non-residents who have not been invited. Policing is private. Residents agree to share the cost of the police because they are the ones who will enjoy the benefits. They will not finance outsiders who might take a free ride. Owning the streets has made citizens keen consumers of security services. Citizens hire the police force and set standards of performance such as frequency of patrols and response times to distress calls. Citizens also establish police salaries and choose recruits. It is hard to measure how satisfied citizens are with their police. But if willingness to pay is a measure of satisfaction, Irvine police are not too shabby. They are the best paid police force in the US.

Another example of private streets can be found in Paris. There are 55 kilometres of private walkways and streets in Paris. This is only 3 percent of the total, but the cleanliness and safety of these areas supports Lyndon Johnson's comment that "The best fertilizer for land is the footprint of its owner." St. Louis residents can vouch for the safety that comes with private streets. In the 1950s, growing crime rates made city residents demand the right to have the city deed them the streets. Residents picked up the tab for street, sewer, and streetlight maintenance, garbage collection, and any security services beyond normal city levels. A resident of one street authority explained that private streets "give people a stronger sense of their own personal stake in a community ... by limiting access to the neighbourhoods, people who have no business there other than to make trouble have a much harder time."

Residents' associations also have the right to limit how people can use their houses. If you put up a boarder who is not a relative or friend, or turn your house into a multi-unit dwelling for transients, concerned neighbours can shut you down. Owning your street gives you an incentive and the means to keep it safe. The result is that crime rates on private streets are at least 50 percent lower than in neighbouring public streets.

Compulsory Police Insurance

Cities that are too timid to privatize the streets but want a privately-run and financed police force need some way of dealing with the common property problem that public streets pose. The solution proposed for private hospitals is to force everyone to take out insurance. Compulsion is the only solution to a common property problem when you refuse to get rid of the problem by privatizing. What you are doing is substituting the compulsion of the state for the compulsion of the private property owner.

HMO-Style Police

What do I have in mind for police? Something like the health maintenance organization in the US. Health maintenance organizations (HMOs) are competing hospitals and clinics that work with insurance companies to keep down costs. In such systems, doctors do not charge the insurance company for each service. Insurance companies pay a flat rate. If the company sends too many demanding patients to the hospital, the hospital renegotiates its contract and charges the company a higher flat rate. The flat rate works its way into insurance fees. These fees may then push consumers to look for new insurers.

This model applies to police forces because it shows how user fees can be worked into a system of public law-enforcement. An HMO-style police force can be organized around precincts. Imagine a city in which citizens under the precinct's protection are sent a monthly protection charge. The charge is sent to all residents, not merely to property owners. To avoid free-riders, all citizens are obliged to pay membership dues for police protection. No one can opt out. To protect members from excessive dues, citizens exercise some form of "shareholder" control over police management. This control comes in one of two forms.

The police remain a government body, and citizens vote to approve salaries and key appointments in the precinct. The other form of control comes by privatizing the existing police force. The police becomes either a for-profit or a non-profit private corporation—just as US hospitals are. These corporations can lose their contracts and be replaced by a competing body, and they are subject to the discipline of their governing boards. An example of such a corporation is the Pinkerton security company. The city of Prague hired hundreds of Pinkerton guards to patrol streets after the communists and their hoodlum enforcers in police uniform were kicked out in 1989. Imagine the Pinkerton company bidding with other security companies to provide services in the same way that Kaiser-Permanente competes with other health companies to provide consumers with health care. The private police hired under competition could be strictly regulated and investigated by an internal affairs unit serving the entire city. This unit can be funded by contributions from all the city's precincts.

The benefit of living in a city where police departments compete is that citizens know how much value they get for their police dollar, something they would not know in a city where the police get paid from a general pot. With police, as with any government department, subsidies from a general pot make it easy for some departments to be inefficient at the expense of others. A police precinct run along the lines of an HMO could not hide its inefficiencies, and citizens would have more choices than they now have in dealing with these inefficiencies.

Predicting exactly how the cost of police service would change under such a regime is difficult because there are few examples to go by. The case of Cap-Rouge on the outskirts of Quebec city tantalizes us with a hint of what could be. Since 1977 Cap-Rouge has bought its police and fire services from neighbouring Sainte-Foy. Between 1990 and 1994, the price Sainte-Foy charged went from $1.1 million to $1.7 million. In 1995, the city of Quebec decided to get into the act and to start bidding to sell its services. Sainte-Foy managed to keep its contract with Cap-Rouge, but the 1995 price fell to $1.4 million. Examples from abroad are equally inspiring. According to Randall Fitzgerald, in the early 1980s the Ohio town of Reminderville was faced with a price increase for public services. The county providing the services wanted to charge $180,000 a year for the use of a patrol car with a guaranteed response time of 45 minutes. Instead of accepting this, the town signed a contract with a private firm which offered a six minute response time with two patrol cars for only

$90,000 a year. Fitzgerald also notes that "in Switzerland the private police firm *Securitas* maintains contracts with more than 30 Swiss townships and villages, patrolling and performing crime-prevention duties like any other city police force, but at a level the Swiss Association of Towns describes as more affordable and efficient."

Another story from Quebec shows how dangerous competition is to police monopolies. If a municipality does not have its own police force, it must pay the provincial government for the protection of the provincial police (the Sûreté du Québec). Feeling the price they paid was too high for the service they got, several small communities banded together to form their own local police forces. Before this genie flew too far out of the bottle, the provincial government decided to outlaw any further competition. Communities without their own police force must depend on the services of the Sûreté. A hardened criminal might chuckle at the sight of the police running its own racket.

Information in User Fees

Few people would suggest that the police are uninterested in the community's welfare. A spirit of public service motivates most police employees. The problem for the police, as for any corporation, is knowing what the community wants. In the private market, the consumer's willingness to pay for a good tells the producer, "You are doing a good job" or "You had better find out more about this consumer's desires." Prices spur the producer to find ways to lower costs, while maintaining service. An HMO-style police might be more willing to innovate than police guaranteed money from the public pot. Innovation might mean hiring private detective agencies to help with investigations or enlisting volunteers for some duties, and relying less on sworn personnel to take care of clerical duties and computer work. A study of Florida police forces by economist Kwabena Gyimah-Brempong suggests that for many tasks in the station, cheaper civilian personnel can substitute for police.

Innovation could also mean the police sends a letter to citizens explaining why it needs to borrow money to pay for a surveillance helicopter, and why citizens should approve the helicopter in a vote. Prices also send a signal to consumers. A high cost of policing might signal that the community is too risky to live in. Citizens would have an incentive to search out communities where protection costs less. The loss of their "clients" might encourage police to find new ways to keep down costs.

Two-tier? Have no Fear

Would HMO-style police lead to a two-tier system of police service in which rich districts get better protection than poor districts? The answer is hard to predict. Rich districts in Canada already have the option of hiring private security guards. Few districts do this. To help poor districts fight crime, rich districts might send money. This is how the International Monetary Fund works. It is a voluntary club of nations that hands out money to developing countries on the condition that they get governments off their entrepreneurs' backs. A voluntary club of rich precincts would help to finance policing in poor precincts, in return for detailed reports on how their gift is being used. In a world of user fees, co-operation and information are the rule. The only guarantee of a subsidy is a region's ability to explain its need and propose reforms that satisfy its donors. With funding guaranteed from general taxes there is less need for explanation and less incentive to correct costly problems. After all, with general financing, "someone else" is paying for the problems.

Keeping Down the Costs of Crime

What is the role of an insurer in HMO-style police? In health, the insurer helps the consumer choose among hospitals and health plans. The insurer also pays money to the incapacitated. It is hard to know whether insurers would appear on the scene described here. Citizens might remain happy paying protection fees directly to the precinct. But it is possible that insurance companies would become middlemen between neighbourhood residents and the police force that protects them. Citizens would shop for the middleman capable of hiring the best private police services, just as investors shop for mutual funds with the best records of placing clients' money. To keep premiums competitive, insurance companies would inform the police force of innovations in battling crime. The police force would have an incentive to listen to the insurer because the insurer pays the force for its services. Any force that did not listen to advice would soon be replaced by a more innovative and flexible security company.

The key in HMO-style police is the added layer of control on the police: the insurer. The insurer is a middleman between citizens and the police. Citizens need a middleman to help them evaluate the protection quality they get. The police need a middleman to help them understand what citizens want. The user fee—in this case the insurance premium—signals how efficiently the insurer keeps risks down and how dangerous the community is.

User Fees Creeping In

Will government ever get around to charging user fees for its police? There are signs that user fees may be on the way. In 1995 Montreal police got 78,745 emergency calls. 95 percent of these were false alarms. Absent-minded residents are pretty much the only targets of the lasers, motion sensors, and vibration detectors that festoon their homes. The Montreal government recently passed a law that allows police to charge a fee for false alarms. The $55 fee for a second false alarm is still less than what it costs police to rush to the rescue, but it will remind homeowners to call off the cavalry in case of false alarm. Toronto charges for police who maintain calm at sporting events and concerts. There is still a long way to go, though, before governments privatize the police force and finance it entirely from consumer insurance premiums.

If I rely heavily on my imagination to paint a picture of cities with private police, it is because there are few examples to go by. It is hard to judge how the costs of police forces would change if cities subcontracted work to the private sector. The police like to keep things in-house, including its forensic laboratories, investigators, computer systems, surveillance units, and bodyguards. No union could hope for a more closed shop. Slightly better evidence on the difference between public and private services comes from studies of fire departments.

Private Fire Protection

Evidence on the benefits of private fire protection comes from Denmark. In a 1983 study, Ole Kristensen found that the private nationwide fire-fighting company run by the Falck family had costs three times lower than those of public fire companies. In Canada, James McDavid has measured the true cost of fire protection. This cost is the sum of property value lost to fire plus the cost of putting fires out. He found that the true cost was 38 percent lower for fire departments that relied on a mix of full-time and part-time workers than for departments that relied entirely on full-time workers. His study does not say that private fire departments are more efficient than public ones. But it says that flexible fire departments are efficient. Some flexibility is allowed under government rule, but even more flexibility would come with privatization.

Should everyone be obliged to subscribe to a basic level of fire protection in a private system? Fire does not respect property lines. Flames and smoke are common property, which means a communal effort is required to fight them. It seems we must all stand in line, passing the bucket. The answer to this question may come from Arizona where the private firm Rural/Metro Fire Department Inc. provides contract fire protection to dozens of communities. Citizens may choose to subscribe. Non-subscribers will still be served by the fire company should their homes burn. The company simply charges these people more than those who pay their insurance up front.

According to the National Fire Protection Association the annual per-capita cost in the 1980s of fire protection in Scottsdale was $25.68. The average cost for cities of similar size, and largely serviced in the US by publicly owned firms, was $50. Scottsdale had the fastest response time to fires and the per capita losses from fire damage which were 32 percent lower than the national average and the lowest in the nation. Remarkably, Rural-Metro accomplished these cost-saving feats while paying its employees on average $1,500 more for starting firefighters than did other firefighting services.

Private fire departments charging citizens directly would probably evolve along the lines of HMOs. HMOs evolved in the medical business to overcome the problem of moral hazard. Doctors who charge a fee for every service may be tempted to convince a patient bursting with rude health that he is ill. Doctors can do this because they are guardians of a large store of information from which ordinary mortals are barred. The doctor can exploit this guardianship to drum up business. The temptation to exploit is a hazard to the doctor's morals. HMOs evolved to protect these morals and the patient's wallet. As I explained earlier, HMOs do not charge direct fees for a range of basic services. There is a similar need to protect citizens from fire departments. In the Roman Republic, Marcus Crassus ran the biggest fire-extinguishing business. His technique was to set a fire, rush his men to the scene, buy the burning building at a knockdown price from the distraught owner, and put the flames out fast. HMO-style fire protection would leave no room for a latter-day Marcus Crassus.

In a private system, fire protection would benefit from user fees in the same way that police protection would benefit. Your insurer working with your HMO-style fire department would give you special discounts for precautions that save the fire department money. At present such measures have to be imposed by force. Citizens do not pay directly for fire protection, so they have no incentive to take measures that would reduce the fire department's costs.

Take the community of Pitt Meadows, British Columbia. Pitt Meadows passed a by-law requiring all buildings, except single-family homes and duplexes, to install fire sprinklers. Sprinklers hold off a fire long enough for fires engines to get to the scene. This by-law spared Pitt Meadows the need to build new stations at the edge of town. This measure has kept the annual cost per person of fire protection at $37.50. The average for the province of British Columbia is $67. If you think the Pitt Meadows sprinkler law is a success, imagine what other innovations could keep down fire protection costs.

Under the present system, innovations forcing people to fireproof their property have to be introduced through the tedious path of law. As William Pollack of the Urban Institute has argued, state-subsidized fire protection service leads to too much fire suppression and too little fire prevention. Under an HMO-style fire department, no laws would be needed to urge fire prevention. Citizens taking the HMO's advice on fire-safety would get a discount on the annual insurance-user fee. Many different incentives could be offered and the HMO could experiment to see which reduce the cost of fire protection most.

The Need to Experiment

Insurance companies have not waited for this book's publication to find ways the police and other organizations such as fire-fighters can improve safety. The Underwriters' Laboratories of Canada is a conduit for information that flows between insurers and fire-fighters. Within their constraints such organizations work well, and it is difficult to measure how much better they would work in a world of user fees and private fire protection. We will never know if we never experiment.

Read On ...

Blomqvist, Ake. *The Health Care Business: International Evidence on Private versus Public Health Care Systems.* Vancouver: The Fraser Institute, 1979.

Fitzgerald, Randall. *When Government Goes Private: Successful Alternatives to Public Services.* San Francisco: Pacific Research Institute, 1998.

Johnson, Les. *The Rebirth of Private Policing.* London: Routledge, 1992.

Gage, Theodore J. "Getting Street-Wise in St. Louis." *Reason Magazine*, August 1981, pp. 18-26.

Gruen, Erich S. *Last Generation of the Roman Republic.* Berkeley: University of California Press, 1974.

Gyimah-Brempong, Kwabena (1989). "Demand for Factors of Production in Municipal Police Departments." *Journal of Urban Economics*, 25:247-259.

Kristensen, Ole (1983). "Public versus Private Provision of Governmental Services: The Case of Danish Fire Protection Services." *Urban Studies*, 20:1-9.

Lemennicier, Bertrand (1997). "La privatisation des rues.' *Journal des economistes et des etudes humaines.* 7:363-374.

McDavid, James C. (1986). "Part-Time Fire Fighters in Canadian Municipalities: Cost and Effectiveness Comparisons." *Canadian Public Administration*, 20:377-387.

Poole, Robert W. Jr. *Cutting Back City Hall.* New York: Universe Books, 1980.

Rochon, Claude. "Tarification des appels d'alarme non fondés." Rapport remis à la Commission de la sécurité publique (séance publique), June 5, 1996.

seven
CITY
DEMOCRACY

A nation may establish a free government, but without municipal institutions it cannot have the spirit of liberty.
—Alexis de Tocqueville, *Democracy in America*

U SER FEES, FREE MARKETS. It seems that nothing could be finer for the modern city. So why am I and a handful of academics the only ones who seem to be turned on by these notions? Why is it that cities have done everything in their power to turn themselves into open fields where any citizen may graze at his neighbour's expense?

Maybe citizens are happy with what they have and don't feel the need to pester their politicians for change. If that's the case then allow me to pull a page from Lenin's repertory of slogans and propaganda. To paraphrase this professor of scoundrels, "the masses are oppressed, only they don't know it." For citizens to properly judge whether to be happy with city hall they need to know the true costs of city government and the alternatives to the style of service they get.

To make use of this knowledge, they need the means to choose the best system. In other words, to keep politicians in line, citizens need information and choice.

Ingredients of Competition

Information and choice are the ingredients of competition. As you might sense, competition is what gives you quality service at low price. When two merchants offer different prices you have choice. For this choice to be meaningful, you need to know that alternatives are out there; you need information. Put information and choice together and you have competition. The high price merchant has to lower his price or close shop.

The communist view was that capitalism oppressed workers by keeping them immobile and ignorant. The communists were right. Capitalists love an ignorant, immobile bunch of consumers. By gouging these thralls with excessive prices, capitalists earn what are known as monopoly profits. But communists did not finish their thought on the matter. Capitalists face a problem: the presence of other capitalists. There is always some annoying rival who will advertise cheaper, better wares. The only response is to advertise twice as hard and lower prices to meet the competition. The result, which is quite unpleasant for capitalists, is that they are continually forcing each other to educate the consumer and provide him with services at prices that are close to cost. But maybe I am slandering the communists' grasp of capitalism. In Russia they allowed no one to compete for power once they got their hands on the government and ran massive state industries for the profit of a champagne-drenched crew of inner party hoodlums. Communists proved themselves the most astute capitalists.

In politics, information and choice play the same critical role as they play in economic markets. Though sometimes hard to believe, we elect politicians to be our servants, not our masters. These servants have a duty similar to that of producers in a private market. Political producers are elected to provide quality government services at a low tax price. A politician is a middleman elected by citizens. This middleman represents citizens in negotiations with public unions. He tries to get the best price possible from contractors hired to build a hospital or a sewer. The cost for his services is our tax bill. Rivals compete for this management post in elections. During the election we shop for the candidate who can provide the best public services at the lowest tax cost. Voters who have information about how much these services cost, and who can choose alternate suppliers check the politician's tendency to overcharge.

Political Profits?

Things go wrong for citizens when their leaders earn too great a profit. Yes, "profit" exists in politics just as it does in commerce. Only it's a lot harder to spot in the public sector because there profit hides under many cloaks. A leader can enjoy the perks of office, give in to public unions without undergoing stress, look good to the public by financing spending with debt, or indulge extremist groups with whom he sympathizes. All of these deviations from the broad public's wishes raise the cost of government and saddle consumers with an excessive tax bill—"excessive" in that the same services could be had at lower cost if citizens were given both more information about how their money is used, and alternatives to choose from.

How do politicians at all levels of government ensure themselves excessive profits? In Canada, as in most other western democracies, part of the trick is to stifle competitive city politics. The town hall is empty. Fewer than 40 percent of citizens vote in city elections. Walk into any pub and the last item you will hear discussed is city hall. The taproom agitator is a distant memory. You almost have to admire a political system that keeps citizens passive without slave camps or a ministry of propaganda. A speech that the tribune Licinius Macer made to the Romans 2,000 years ago describes city politics today:

"You have been stripped of every privilege your forefathers left you except your ballots, and by them, you who once chose your defenders now choose your masters."

The Death of City Politics

Politicians neutered Canadian city politics because they understood that cities are geysers of information and choice. As local governments do most of the taxing and spending, it is easy for citizens to judge whether their governments do a good job. All they have to do is look across the municipal border at how well governments are performing there. If parents in the neighbouring county are paying less tax and getting better education for their children, I will ask my elected representative some hard questions. Putting power close to the people—known as "decentralization"—gives them a standard of comparison. It provides the evidence citizens need to call their leaders to account. Once people see what life is like on the "other side," they will not settle for less. As that World War I song put it, "How are 'ya going to keep 'em down on the farm, after they've seen Paree?"

If my representative fails to answer my questions and proves obtuse on other matters, I might decide to sell my house and cross the local border. If enough people leave, or simply threaten to leave, the government will have to clean up its act. Otherwise it risks a brain drain of its best people. The political pressure informed citizens exert on their leaders by threatening to leave is known as "voting-with-your-feet." This combination of information and choice is lethal for slack politicians. If they do not watch what they do, they will be outcompeted by neighbouring governments. This fear of political competition explains why the Soviet Union jammed radio signals and surrounded its people with concertina wire and guard dogs. These measures kept people ignorant and immobile.

How do Canada's politicians protect themselves from the threat of vibrant city democracy? The constitution of 1867, also known as the

British North America Act, provided the first defence by refusing to recognize municipal governments. Provincial legislatures stepped into the vacuum and grabbed the power to incorporate municipalities. Provinces used their whip hand to suppress the "general competence" of cities. General competence of municipal government is "the right to take an action on behalf of its local community, that is not specifically barred to it." Without this competence, municipalities must sit by while provinces decide how much leash they will get to raise revenue, pass by-laws, and reform local democracy. It comes as no surprise that cities have not advanced on any of these fronts. Since the turn of the century, they have not stopped retreating.

Keeping User Fees in the Closet

First, take a look at city finances. What strikes you is that cities either have little power or little incentive to charge user fees for their services. Whether a user fee is charged for water or transportation is usually up to the province. Even when cities have the right to charge fees, they have little incentive because the province offers subsidies for the city service. The main source of revenue cities are allowed is taxing property.

Politicians from Ottawa and the province have little choice but to suppress user fees. If city dwellers paid the true price of the services they consume as they consume them, they would start asking questions. An honest user fee would force the question, "Why does it cost $30 to ride the Vancouver SkyTrain?" or "Why is my sewer bill so high?" Fees educate the consumer. Dishing out money to pay for the service makes you think. Could this be done more cheaply? The moment voters start asking questions is the moment they start demanding power. The last thing the provinces and Ottawa want is to lose their powers to the city. Forbidding user fees has been a way of squelching such demands.

Evidence in support of this notion comes from the work of economist John Matsusaka of the University of Southern California. He analyzed the 26 US states where citizens have the power to initiate their own laws. Where citizens had the power of initiative, they demanded (all other things constant) that user fees be 12 percent higher and general taxes 12 percent lower than in states without the initiative. Citizens in initiative states also forced government spending to be decentralized to local government. One way to read these results is that citizens like fees because fees provide information about leaders. And once they get user fees, they want to make sure that the power to make political decisions stays close to the people.

Subsidies Kill Information and Choice

The second striking feature of city finances is how much moolah cities get from higher levels of government. A subsidy from a higher level of government is an arrow through the heart of city politics. The subsidy hides how well local politicians perform and turns voters into profligate, uncritical consumers of city services. Ian Preston and Michael Ridge, economists at London's Institute for Fiscal Studies, found that subsidies from higher levels of government boost voter demand for city services. This should not happen if voters understand that they will pay for the subsidy with their taxes. The authors concluded that the subsidy hides the true cost of local services. This tricks voters into demanding more from the government than they would if they paid the full price directly and immediately.

Consider the Montreal subway. The province of Quebec covers most of the subway's capital costs and an important minority of its operating costs. This allows the Metros' managers to give in to unions and bumble in their search to lower costs. City residents have no incentive to complain because citizens of the cities of Quebec, Chicoutimi, and Riviere-du-Loup, to name a few, pick up the tab. Vancouverites, Calgarians, Kingstonians, and just about everyone else west of Quebec also chips in. According to economists Isabella Horry and

Michael Walker, in 1990, Ontario, Albert and British Columbia provided each Quebec citizen with $696 dollars of federal subsidy per year. So why should Montrealers' hair turn grey from worrying about Metro costs? Citizens of other towns have little reason to complain. As the Ontario Economic Council put it as far back as 1969:

> Through the development of a complex transfer system, each level of government can influence the nature and scope of the services provided, take a share in the political rewards, maintain the fiction of autonomy, and have a convenient excuse for avoiding any criticism for inadequate services. The only drawback is that the public never knows who is responsible for what or how much the services provided really cost.

This passage describes the mind-numbing effect of subsidies. By removing our incentive to inform ourselves about how leaders are doing their jobs, subsidies work better than any Soviet equipment for jamming radio signals could. Subsidies jam the signals in our minds.

What the above passage does not mention is that subsidies also kill a citizen's ability to vote with his feet. In a world without subsidies, citizens can move to the community that gives better service for less tax cost. In a world of subsidies, there is no place to run. The provincial subsidy comes from every community in the province. Money from the province converts a city tax into a province-wide tax from which there is no escape. What brilliant insight by our provincial leaders! They understood that if citizens voted too easily with their feet, poorly-managed communities would demand the democratic power needed to put their local leaders in place. A subsidy falls like snow on these demands, freezing and burying them while leaders from higher levels of government stay warm and worry-free in their citadels.

Since subsidies contribute an average of 45 percent to Canadian city finances, the sceptical reader might ask whether a practice that is so widespread can be as malign as I say it is. Let us back off a few feet from this critique and admit that, on the surface, there are reasons why subsidies appear to be good for the city. For example, how is a city to finance services that benefit out-of-town drivers? City roads are the prime example. In his survey of infrastructures, US economist Edward Gramlich explains that perhaps 30 percent of drivers who benefit from expressways and inter-city highways live elsewhere. This is probably an upper limit of any estimated percentage of city traffic consisting of people who do not live there. This means that a 30 percent subsidy from a higher level of government ensures that these outsiders pay their share of the city's street costs.

I say "on the surface" because if you have been following me on this canter down the urban range, you will remember that cities could charge a direct fee for anyone who drives their streets. User fees nab the user and do away with the need for subsidies. Almost every argument in favour of city subsidies is based on the notion that outsiders will poach those services for which a city has trouble charging directly. When users cannot be identified or barred from the service, the provincial government must set things right with taxes and subsidies. The province compensates the city for the damage that poachers do, by taxing the poachers on their home turf through provincial income tax.

A city leader seduced by this argument stops looking for ways to impose user fees and turn poachers into paying consumers. Part of the success story of private markets is the clever search for ways to make consumers pay. Imagine what television would look like now if in 1930 governments had agreed to subsidize TV stations on the grounds that anyone with an antenna can poach the TV signal. Technology would have stood still. The subsidy would have excused TV stations from the need to sell advertising. The subsidy would have killed the incentive for scientists to invent cable and satellite transmission with electronic decoders. All these advances were made to ensure that those who watch TV pay for their entertainment. No such innovation would have been needed had higher levels of government promised to pick up the tab for TV stations the way they do for cities.

Don't subsidies redistribute money and ensure that the poor are relieved from paying for city services? Maybe. Subsidies are paid for by taxes. Taxes are like hot potatoes that get passed around. The poor man who does not pay for water at home may pay for it when he buys coffee downtown, where tax-paying businesses pass the cost on to consumers. These subtleties aside, there is still the problem that subsidies to cities help not just the poor, but anyone who rides the bus or puts out his garbage. If you want to help the poor, as I explained a few chapters back, give them help directly. Do not filter that aid through city hall where the coins land on everyone, poor and rich.

Property Taxes

Property taxes share the information and choice-killing properties of subsidies. The property tax allows cities to provide services without charging for them directly. The tax can also make it hard to vote with your feet, provided the city is big enough. This might explain why Canadian cities have a tendency to amalgamate and grow like fungus. The larger the city, the harder it is for citizens to see what city leaders are up to and to escape their depredations.

In 1994, competition between the city of Toronto and its suburbs showed how badly politicians are rankled when citizens are free to move where they please. The problem facing Toronto city hall was that for years it squandered money to run a complicated "two-tier" government. Both tiers seem to have been designed for the benefit of special interest groups and inefficient public bureaucracies. To feed this Moloch, councillors raised taxes beyond the endurance of businesses and middle-class property owners. In the 1980s and 1990s, these groups fled to the suburbs. In the suburbs taxes were low, and the regulations made sense.

Toronto councillors faced the sickening prospect of having to lower their taxes, end ridiculous zoning laws, and cut spending on goodies for noisy special interests. Short of putting an iron curtain around the city, there seemed no other way of keeping its citizens from moving. But in their desperation, Toronto councillors came up with an elegant defence against competition. Why not force the suburbs to raise their taxes? The roundabout way of doing this was to convince the provincial government to levy most of the municipal taxes. Toronto politicians pleaded with the province to shift the cost of running education from the city tax base to the provincial tax rolls.

With property taxes out of municipal hands, no neighbouring community could offer citizens a better tax deal than Toronto. Everyone in Ontario would pay the same provincial rate of property tax no matter how good or bad their public services were. One inescapable tax rate over the province would put a convenient end to what Toronto politicians were calling "unfair tax competition" from the suburbs.

Hankering for a common tax rate and an end to tax competition is known in clinical circles as "tax harmonization envy." Tax harmony is a nice expression for an ugly practice for which the European Community has written the book. As the 1992 date for European free trade approached, it dawned on leaders that their tax revenues were in danger. What if France decided to set its GST at half the German rate? Germans would shop in France and the German government would lose tax revenue. To avoid this risk six members of the Community agreed to harmonize their GST rates at 15 percent. Toronto politicians wanted to protect themselves from the same risk of losing revenue by forcing neighbouring cities and suburbs to keep their taxes high.

Special Purpose Killers of Democracy

Where subsidies and property taxes have not sufficed to neuter city politics, special purpose boards and commissions have stepped in to take up the challenge. These shady entities were hatched at the turn of the century out of social activism and special interest pleadings. The view among the "elites" back then was that city services were too complicated for citizens to have much say in their management. In 1890, Goldwin Smith, a prominent municipal reformer in Toronto, explained that "a city is simply a densely peopled district in need of a specially skilled administration."

Anyone capable of mouthing such a comment would have been impermeable to de Tocqueville's insight that city politics are the building blocks of democracy. Reformers with equally dense hides took it on themselves to eliminate mass politics from city government. As Richard and Susan Tindal note in the leading text on local government in Canada: "Their rallying cry was 'there's no political way to build a road.'" The Tindals add that "This statement is true, as far as the technical requirements of paving materials and building standards. But the decision on where to build a road is certainly political.... The decision on whether to allocate limited funds to roads (or transportation) versus such other competing needs as waste management, fire protection or public housing is also political."

Special purpose boards and commissions moved decisions about roads, police, and sewers from the public arena to the back room. Boards and commissions replaced mass politics with special interest group politics. As Jack Masson explains in his survey of Alberta municipal governments, "Boards, commissions and committees do not take particular functions out of politics; rather they remove these functions from the control and scrutiny of the citizenry to those of special interests in the community."

Today the variety of boards and commissions is pretty much the same as at the turn of the century. School boards, police commissions, library boards, family and children's services, conservation authorities, transit and utility commissions and others have clung to the ship of city government like immortal barnacles. Municipal economist Harry Kitchen explains the problem with these encrustations:

> Of the many boards and commissions in existence, a large number enjoy considerable autonomy and financial independence. In fact, many of these bodies are little governments in themselves ... independent and in no way subordinate to elected politicians. This proliferation of decision-making bodies ... creates an environment over which citizens have little control and hence, is politically inefficient. For many of these special-purpose bodies, there is no direct link between the policy-making body and hence, the body making expenditures.... Whenever expenditure and revenue decisions are made independently, there is no reason to believe that the system is as accountable as it should be ... if accountability in decision making is lacking, the system is unlikely to allocate its resources efficiently across competing services.... Perhaps the most serious problem encountered with boards and commissions is the extent to which these bodies appropriate significant portions of local government revenue ... in one estimate of Metropolitan Toronto, for example, it was noted that approximately 60 percent of net expenditures financed from own-source revenues went to special purpose bodies. (p. 14)

The Roads to City Democracy

Unravelling the folly of a century of repression is not going to be easy. But it has to be done. City government is a sleeping giant waiting for a nudge. When it wakes, it will force politicians at every level to reduce their takings from government. Leaders will then start working more for the public than for those specialized feeders who see government as a giant cow with millions of udders.

The benefits that come from making politicians accountable to their citizens are the same sort that came to shareholders who experienced the leveraged buyout revolution of the 1980s. Leveraged buyouts were researched and developed by a group of financiers at Drexel Burnham and Lambert of Wall Street. Under the leadership of Michael Milken, this group brought together investors who spotted a company that was poorly managed with the company's desperate shareholders. Milken raised money for investors so that they could buy out the shareholders and turf out inefficient managers who had been bottling up the company's potential. Research in the 1990s shows that these buyouts raised the value of the shareholders being bought out. There is some evidence that it also raised that stock of investors who are doing the buying, though the verdict is still out on this point. The leveraged buyout reminded managers that if they abused their position, they could be dismissed. This is the same message we need to send our politicians.

But which politicians do we target? As I have explained, provincial subsidies force every city to pay for every other city's services, making it impossible for citizens to relate the quality of service to service cost. The first step in reviving city democracy is to get the province out of the business of giving subsidies to cities. Once citizens realize how much local services really cost, they will demand change. If they don't like the change they get, they will move to a different neighbourhood or city.

IMF at Home

Note that I am not saying that subsidies between cities should end. Subsidies are not bad, provided city residents know they are getting them or giving them. Citizens would have this knowledge if Canada became a federation of thousands of municipal governments, like Switzerland's federation of over 3,000 communes. A federation of many small governments would keep citizens up-to-date on how their money is spent. Ottawa and the provinces could no longer act as screens between the citizens who pay and the citizens who play. In a decentralized state, a city wanting help would have to ask the other cities directly. These cities, under the watchful eye of a municipal electorate, would knock their heads together to come up with an aid package that stood a chance of pulling the poor city out of misery.

This is what the IMF does. It is a voluntary club of nations that hands out money to developing countries. The money comes with strings attached. The IMF uses these strings to yank governments of developing countries off their entrepreneurs' backs. Canadian cities would have an interest in seeing that the same thing happens here. In a decentralized state, the cost of transfers to other cities would appear on the budgets of the cities who pay. Citizens would want to make sure the transfer dollars they are giving away are being spent productively.

The information these citizens need to make up their minds about the wise use of transfer payments would come courtesy of the politicians of poor cities. These politicians would have to explain why they need money, what they are going to do with it, and how well they managed money they got last year. In other words, decentralization would set off an explosion of information. It would force citizens to come to an understanding with each other. In a centralized state, some people use the central government to snatch money away from others. In a decentralized state, this poaching is not possible. Groups needing help have to come face-to-face with the groups giving help, and must explain why they need it.

Shareholder Democracy

Replacing property taxes with user fees is the next step on the road to reviving city democracy. The benefits from this step are similar to the benefits of getting rid of provincial subsidies: more information and mobility for citizens. Along with user fees should come a privatization of most city services. As I suggested in earlier chapters, the costs of operating these services privately may fall by as much as 30 percent. This is reason enough for wedding privatization to user fees, but as I am now rambling on about democracy, I should ramble to the point, which is that privatization is a form of democracy.

Imagine how citizen attitudes would change if instead of being passive "stakeholders" they became active shareholders in city services. The notion of transferring ownership of public resources to the public is not discussed in polite political circles here. As Lord Raglan said after the charge of the Light Brigade, "It isn't done." When Canadian politicians privatize, they sell a company and rake in the revenues, so that no part of their power is dissipated to the people.

As Queen's Business School professors Lewis Johnson and Bohumír Pazderka explain, the Czech Republic is one of the few countries that has dared to privatize its industries by placing them directly in the people's hands. It now has a stable democracy, where citizens take an interest in how the economy is managed. They had better. They are part owners. What would Czech-style privatization do for city dwellers in Canada? All of a sudden you would put city service managers under the scrutiny of thousands of citizens. These citizens would convene at shareholder meetings to oust poor managers. Citizen-shareholders would care about the bottom line and ensure that their companies are keeping costs low. Those citizens not caring to involve themselves directly could put their shares into the hands of a mutual fund manager. This manager would discipline city managers not taking good care of his client's interests. The citizen unhappy with his fund manager could switch to another. In other words, citizen shareholders get to vote as often as they like. They are not restricted to voting once every two or four years for a city council itself powerless over special purpose boards and commissions. No wonder leaders do not want to "give away" the resources of the state.

To some readers, the democratic reforms I am proposing may seem like killing the patient to heal the sickness. Will anything be left for cities to govern if they follow my advice? The answer is "plenty." Think of a country club. It is privately owned, but governed by a board of owners who vote on measures everyone must follow. The private owners of these clubs want a common space in which to meet and play. Though this space is privately owned, it is open to all members. Even "private" common properties need rules moderating members' use of the common space.

The city of Irvine in California is privately owned, but it is nonetheless governed by many separate owners' associations. The difference between Irvine's common space and the common space of most other cities lies in how people agree on its use. No owner's association serves more than 30,000. They are typically much smaller. This allows residents to move easily from one association to the other if they do not like the kinds of agreements being reached. Ease of movement guarantees that people will cluster into associations with people of similar mind. In this system, neighbourhoods become clubs of like-minded individuals where laws are arrived at by consensus, not by the fractious methods necessary in mega-cities such as Toronto or Halifax. Privatizing large parts of what is now under city government control does not kill the need for city government. Privatizing simply changes the way people hammer out solutions to common problems.

Before we can taste any of these democratic goodies, we need some way of letting politicians know these are what we want. Sending the message is hard because ordinary citizens do not have the time to lobby their leaders. There always seems to be a special interest group ready to squash any reform that threatens to pull the group's hand out of the public cookie jar. The best method devised so far for flanking special interest groups and getting government to reform is direct democracy.

Economist John Matsusaka has shown that in the US citizens able to propose laws directly tend to demand user fees and decentralization. The only problem is that to achieve direct democracy you need cooperative leaders. Some signs of cooperation are appearing in populist governments, such as those in Alberta and Ontario. At the federal level, the Reform Party has spoken out in favour of direct democracy. How much power politicians put into our hands remains to be seen. Once we get power, we might discover that we don't need leaders to make all our decisions. We might also pull government down to eye level by reviving city politics and shifting finances away from Ottawa and the provinces. Once this starts happening, we will get the ideal cities I have been describing.

Read On ...

Gramlich, Edward M. (1994). "Infrastructure Investment: A Review Essay." *Journal of Economic Literature*, 32:1176-1196.

Johnson, Lewis and Bohumir Pazderka. *Its No Gamble: The Economic and Social Benefits of Stock Markets.* Vancouver: The Fraser Institute, 1995.

Horry, Isabella, and Michael Walker. *Government Spending Facts 2.* Vancouver: Fraser Institute, 1994.

Kitchen, Harry (1992). "Efficient Delivery of Local Government Services." Kingston: Industrial Relations Library, Discussion Paper No. 93-15.

Masson, Jack. *Alberta's Local Governments and their Politics.* Edmonton: University of Alberta Press, 1985.

Matsusaka, John G. (1995). "Fiscal Effect of the Voter Initiative: Evidence from the Last 30 Years." *Journal of Political Economy*, 103:587-623.

Palda, Filip. *Here the People Rule: A Toolbook for Reforming Democracy.* Minnesota: Paragon House Publishers, 1997.

Preston, Ian and Michael Ridge (1995). "Demand for Local Public Spending: Evidence from British Social Attitudes Survey." *The Economic Journal*, 105:644-660.

Tindall, Richard C., and Susan Nobes Tindall. *Local Government in Canada: Fourth Edition.* Toronto: McGraw-Hill, 1995.

Treff, Karin and David B. Perry. *Finances of the Nation 1996.* Toronto: Canadian Tax Foundation, 1997.

eight
CONCLUSION

Bounty is a bottomless pit. For how can it be anything else, when those who have got accustomed to being subsidized are bound to want more, and persons who have never been at the receiving end want to get there?
—Cicero, *On Duties*

C ITIES WERE INVENTED TO DEFEAT DISTANCE and bring varied people together. People need each other in more ways than the family can provide. They need to exchange ideas, goods, and services with friends and strangers. The search for an exchange that benefits both sides goes best when many traders find themselves in the same spot. This spot is called a market. Cities provide a permanent spot to meet and exchange valuables. Permanence allows merchants and consumers to learn who is trustworthy and where to find the best buys. In sum, cities exist to connect people to each other. To concentrate people successfully in a small space you need special technologies such as city streets, sewers, water mains, police and fire protection, sanitation, and public transport. These inventions allow millions to cram into and live in a few hundred hectares in the battle against distance.

Prices are Lighthouses

Organizing this cramming is quite a feat. Among countless other concerns, you have to make sure that streets don't become clogged and that citizens moderate their production of garbage. Unregulated markets solve these problems with the help of prices. Prices sort the wheat from the chaff. If it costs money to drive downtown, then people will ask themselves, "Do I really need to drive, or should I take the subway? Maybe I shouldn't even be living in the suburbs but in a downtown flat instead." When prices reflect how scarce a resource is and how much certain people value that resource, consumers are forced to ask themselves meaningful questions about where they live and their use of city services.

An unregulated city will tend to make suburban living expensive and city living cheap because the cost of infrastructure to support a suburbanite is greater than the cost of infrastructure to support a city dweller. This truth follows from the fact that suburbs are spread out and require more capital investment per resident. Consider Surrey, British Columbia, and Paris, France. Both cities have about 1,600 kilometres of roads. Surrey has a population of 300,000. Paris has more than ten times that number. Guess which city has a lower cost of infrastructure per resident?

Scrambling the Signals

High-cost, spread out cities such as Surrey exist because modern governments have hidden the cost of them. The disguise comes in the form of property taxes and provincial subsidies. These funds come from a central pot and are used to provide us with "free" or "cheap" access to city services such as roads, transit, and water. We use these services without paying directly for them. The result is like forcing us into a smorgasbord. We pay an entry fee, like it or not, and sit before a banquet table. The result is an unwanted feast. What grabs you about smorgasbords is that the banquet table belongs to no one in particular. It is a common pasture where everyone grazes without restriction. Subsidies convert private property into common grazing ground. In the conversion, we lose the respect and restraint that private property instills in owners and passers-by.

The obvious signs of our unrestricted grazing are congested streets and an excessive demand on almost all city resources. Other signs are more subtle. Subsidies hide the difference in cost between living at the centre of the city and living at the edge. A road subsidy makes suburban life as cheap as city life. The result is that cities sprawl instead of rising, as they should. Property taxes work the same sort of mischief. These taxes allow the city to fund specific services, free of direct charge, from a central pot of revenues. By filling this central pot, subsidies and property taxes disconnect the user from the cost, and scramble the signals that prices should send in the development of the city.

A lack of user fees also flattens the city by creating a demand for low-density zoning laws. There are many possible explanations for the sprawl of North America cities. One possible reason is that people pay for their central city services out of a common pot of property taxes. This means that people living in low-cost housing pay less tax for the same city services as people living in high-cost housing. Citizens who did not like this style of indirect subsidy fled to suburban communities where like flocked with like and no hidden transfers took place through central financing. To prevent residents of low-cost housing from following them to the suburbs, high-cost dwellers demanded zoning laws that limited how many dwelling units could be built on a parcel of land. The result is the spread-out look of suburbs.

Low density zoning laws have an additional sweetener: they keep out the competition. The last thing established residents want is to see their house prices fall because a new high-rise offers shoppers a cheaper way of living in the suburbs. A number of US studies confirm that zoning keeps the price of housing artificially high by forbidding high-density use of land. There are, of course, legitimate reasons for zoning. The main reason is to protect residents from seeing the value of their property degraded by unsightly, noisy, or polluting structures. But as US economists Denis Mills and Hamilton explain, this type of nuisance is minimal.

User Fees as Property Rights

With what do you replace a subsidy or a property tax? The answer may be user fees. In this book, I have tried to show how almost every city service from roads to police can be charged for. User fees by themselves, though, may do harm if they are not set close to the costs of producing city services. To keep costs down, it is important to privatize the production of these services and to allow private producers to compete with each other.

Privatization is a reshuffling of property rights leading to low-cost production. Costs are lower under private ownership because the owners get to pocket the profits. The right to profits gives owners an incentive to watch over their company's managers to ensure that costs remain low and innovations keep coming. When city hall runs the bus, you the taxpayer finance the operation but have no direct say in how it is run. The final word goes to administrators and unions. These group are not allowed to pocket the profits, so they have little incentive to keep costs down. In fact, unions want to see labour costs rise because this is how they enrich themselves. They lobby for elevated salaries which are then extracted from the captive taxpayer. It's a nice racket.

Subsidies and property taxes keep demand for public service high. This high demand allows unions to swell their ranks. They gouge citizens by keeping costs high, but citizens have trouble complaining because property taxes and subsidies obscure the costs of individual city services. In a world of user fees, such a vanishing act is not possible. Mix in some competition and no single union can hold users of the service captive.

Looking at the modern city's problem's in this way simplifies the search for a solution. The mark of a city in trouble is a lack of respect for private property. Subsidies, property taxes, and monopolies are cancers that infiltrate the city's fibre. Cities bring these afflictions on themselves by being stationary centres of wealth. No longer do marauders need to roam the caravan routes in search of victims. Marauders have taken up residence around the stationary caravan we call the city. Whether a city is stationary or mobile, marauders do the same sort of damage. They spread chaos.

The signs of city chaos are hard for us to see because we are children of the storm. Growing up in traffic jams and sprawling suburbs makes it hard to think of these phenomena as signs of a slow motion battle between the order imposed by property rights and the chaos spread by forces who want to steal those rights. To save the city, we need to restore respect for property.

Decentralization as Property Rights

The struggle between predators and prey over a city's resources is not as stark as it sounds. Almost all of us take on both roles. We are preyed upon, and we prey upon others. This is not a contest between good and evil. It is a contest that pits citizen against citizen in subtle and bewildering ways that make it hard know who comes out on top. This is usually what happens when reformers and well-meaning citizens concentrate power in the hands of politicians. Citizens make demands that others pay for. Politicians go along because as the middlemen who broker these deals they get a cut of the action. These dealings go on as long as citizens are blind to the true costs of their demands and are deprived of the means to control their leaders.

By decentralizing power to the lowest possible level and giving citizens the power to propose laws directly, much of the struggle that now degrades the city will end. Decentralization means that a small area raises its own revenues and spends it own money, without receiving subsidies or paying taxes to a higher level of government. Citizens in a decentralized state can move to communities of like-minded citizens. Because government comes down to eye level citizens can control their leaders. Often they do away with leaders and simply vote on community issues directly.

The common views and information on government that exist in such a community are a means of restoring respect for property. Think of a country club. Similar people use it. Their common outlook keeps them from abusing it. Communities such as these may have little need for user fees because everyone there agrees to control himself. Communities that have not yet achieved this level of harmony can stop citizens from beating up on each other by imposing full user fees and privatizing or contracting out city services.

Asking the Right Questions

What about schooling and public housing? Schooling alone swallows up half the revenues that cities raise through their property taxes. I have ignored schooling in this book because it has little to do with city development. Cities exist to bring people together. The business of city government is to make sure this rapprochement occurs. Schools should have no greater claim on the city's budget than shoe stores. Schooling bears no clear relation to the structure of the city. It is also an enterprise best left in private hands, as Edwin West has shown in his classic analysis of public education. The same holds true for housing. If these dismissals seem cavalier and cruel to the poor then please go back a few chapters to my discussion of how the poor should be helped in a city of user fees and little government meddling.

I have no doubt forgotten to discuss other aspects of city policy. But at this point, I consider my duty done. The purpose of this tour was to arm you with questions: Does the government's proposal violate the property rights of city dwellers? How will this violation warp city development? Once you learn to ask these, you will spot whether the city's potential is being stifled, and you will no longer need a guide on your tour of the urban range.

Read On ...

Goldberg, Michael and Peter Horwood. *Zoning: Its Costs and Relevance for the 1980's.* Vancouver: Fraser Institute, 1980.

West, Edwin G., *Education and the State: A Study in Political Economy.* London: Institute for Economic Affairs, 1965.

Mills, Edwin S. and Bruce W. Hamilton. *Urban Economics, 4th Edition.* Boston: Scott, Foresman and Company, 1989.